Wyggeston and Queen Elizabeth I College

Please return the book on or before the last date shown below

1 0 OCT 2000

_ 1 DEC 2000

Coming on Strong
New Writing from the Royal Court Theatre

NICK GROSSO

Nick Grosso is twenty-six. He was born in London and attended Hampstead Comprehensive School in London. In 1993 he had a monologue, *Mam Don't*, produced by the Royal Court Young People's Theatre and put on at the Commonwealth Institute, London, where it was directed by Roxana Silbert. He also had a poem exhibited at the 'Poetry on Walls' exhibition at Cooltan Arts, London. His first play, *Peaches*, was produced by the Royal Court Theatre in association with the Royal National Theatre Studio and put on at the Royal Court Theatre Upstairs, London, in 1994, directed by James Macdonald. He is currently under commission to write one stage- and one screenplay and has been offered the writer's residency at the Royal National Theatre Studio for later this year.

MICHAEL WYNNE

Michael Wynne was born and brought up in Birkenhead. He came to London in 1991 to study politics at Queen Mary and Westfield College and wrote *The Knocky* in his final year. Since graduating in the summer of 1994, *The Knocky* has been produced twice at the Royal Court, first in October as part of the Young Writers' Festival and then in a larger production in February 1995, which also went on tour. He has just been commissioned by the Royal Court to write another play. He is now twenty-two.

REBECCA PRICHARD

Rebecca Prichard was born in 1971 and grew up in Essex. She studied drama at Exeter University and graduated in 1993. Since writing *Essex Girls* she has written another, short, play for the Royal Court Young People's Theatre and is currently under commission by the Royal Court to write her second full-length play.

KEVIN COYLE

Kevin Coyle was born in Derry in 1977. He will complete his A-levels in the summer of 1996 at St. Columb's College, Derry. *Corner Boys* is his first play.

Coming on Strong

New Writing from the Royal Court Theatre

Peaches
NICK GROSSO

The Knocky
MICHAEL WYNNE

Essex Girls
REBECCA PRICHARD

Corner Boys
KEVIN COYLE

Preface by Stephen Daldry
Introduction by Dominic Tickell

faber and faber
LONDON · BOSTON

First published in 1995
by Faber and Faber Limited
3 Queen Square London WC1N 3AU

Photoset by Parker Typesetting Service, Leicester
Printed in England by Clays Ltd, St Ives plc

Contents

Preface

In 1976 Gerald Chapman, the newly appointed Director
of the Young People's Theatre Scheme, organized a
meeting in one of the half derelict garages at the back of
the theatre to gauge interest in creating a youth theatre. A
youthful Simon Curtis (later to become Deputy Director of
the Royal Court and now Executive Producer of the BBC's
Drama Group series) turned up, as did about eight or nine
others. Originally calling themselves 'The Activists' they
became the Royal Court's Youth Theatre which over the
past twenty years has grown into one of the country's
most vital and important sources of new talent.

One of the key programmes organized by the Young
People's Theatre has been the Young Writer's Festival
which has been at the very heart of the Court's policy of
developing and encouraging young people to write for the
stage since 1973. It has been an extraordinary success
story, not just in terms of the writers who have emerged
from the process, but also the opportunity to flourish
which has been given to a wide diversity of individuals
from communities throughout the country who may have
had no previous contact with theatre.

In the autumn of 1994 and spring of 1995, the Court
was able to continue this process of development by
doubling the number of productions in the Theatre
Upstairs and focusing the policy on young writers. The
huge success of this season pays testimony to the fact that
there is a growing urgency in young people to express
themselves through dramatic writing and the only crisis in
new writing is one of opportunity. The season was
achieved with the key support of the Jerwood Foundation

and the National Theatre Studio who joined us in celebrating the daring and vivacity of the new playwrights of today.

I am delighted that the writers who have emerged through the Young People's Theatre, and in particular the Young Writer's Festival, are now being published. I sincerely hope that you share our enthusiasm for these plays and, just as importantly, appreciate the process by which they have emerged.

Stephen Daldry
Artistic Director, Royal Court Theatre
July 1995

Introduction

All of the plays featured in this volume have been performed at the Royal Court Theatre in London and the playwrights have all attended developmental playwriting workshops provided by the Royal Court and, more specifically, by the Royal Court Young People's Theatre. *Coming on Strong* – the title taken from the 1994 Young Writer's Festival – is therefore an ambassador for the work of the Young People's Theatre.

Established in 1965, the Royal Court Young People's Theatre is now thirty years old. Over the past three decades our work has developed into five central areas:
- Youth Theatre, at the heart of which lies the Writers' Group
- Royal Court/Marks & Spencer Young Writers' Festival
- Community programme
- Work with the unemployed
- Productions of plays for Small Scale Touring.

Corner Boys, *Essex Girls* and *The Knocky* (which also toured to the east of England) all emerged from the workshops run during the 1993–94 Young Writers' Festival. *Peaches* was written while Nick Grosso was attending the Writers' Group at the Young People's Theatre.

The Youth Theatre
The Young People's Theatre is a department of the Royal Court Theatre. As such it is fundamental for us to create, commission and inspire new work which will address 'the problems and possibilities of our times'.

The Royal Court Young People's Theatre was formed in

1965 to encourage a young audience into the Royal Court Theatre. This continues to be one of our aims but the organization has grown enormously since its inception. As well as being the department responsible for the Royal Court's youth work, we now organize the theatre's community outreach work and play a part in the education work, led by Elyse Dodgson.

In 1986 the Young People's Theatre left the comparatively rarefied air of Sloane Square and moved to the Portobello Road. This move enabled us to forge relationships with young people from the widely diverse ethnic groups based in the area and to generate new plays from writers exploring and celebrating their various cultural histories and traditions.

At the core of our work lies the belief that drama and theatre can equip young people with life and citizenship skills as well as encouraging and developing intellectual ability and appetite. Our approach to practical drama and theatre workshops provides a context in which the participants can develop and experiment with their ideas and preoccupations. The approach we adopt is rigorous and the workshops are designed to be constructive, creative and fun. All young people are able to join our youth theatre and can take part in the various projects that we offer. We have an active outreach policy which concentrates on attracting young people to work with us from sections of the community currently under-represented in the field – just one aspect of our work funded by the Royal Borough of Kensington and Chelsea.

Led by a professional writer, the Youth Theatre runs a permanent group for young people who wish to write for the theatre. Andrew Alty became the Writers' Tutor in 1992 and the post has recently been taken over by Tamsin Oglesby. The workshops are not designed to produce a generation of professional playwrights but to enable those who wish to explore the world through the medium of playwriting to do so. However, it is the aim of the workshop to encourage each member to fully realize their potential as a writer.

The Writers' Group has an almost mythical status in the Youth Theatre. Under Andrew's expert tutelage a growing confidence has been engendered in all those attending the group. Specific writing exercises will be set that might require the participants to think about character, place or structure and the second half of the evening devoted to discussing and workshopping pieces of work generated by members of the group. This robust approach exists within a supportive framework which ensures that the writers see comment by others as constructive. Nick Grosso chose to expose himself to this type of discussion and sympathetic criticism while he was writing *Peaches*.

The Royal Court/Marks & Spencer Young Writers' Festival

The Young Writers' Festival began life in 1972 and was the first of its kind in the UK or, possibly, the world. The festival was originally production based. That meant that young people were invited to send in scripts to the Royal Court for consideration, some of which would be developed and produced. One of the most successful, in production terms, was Andrea Dunbar's *Rita, Sue and Bob Too*, which was later adapted for the screen.

In 1987, the then Director of the Young People's Theatre, Elyse Dodgson, added a significant new dimension to the work by introducing workshops which aim to encourage all young people (under the age of twenty-three) to write for the theatre. In order to facilitate this process, professional playwrights, actors and directors associated with the Royal Court support the writers as they develop their scripts.

The underlying principles of the festival echo those of the Young People's Theatre and to this end the participation of young people from all sections of society is encouraged.

During each festival we collaborate with other arts organizations to provide playwriting workshops in different parts of the UK. For the 1994 festival, our efforts were concentrated in London and Northern Ireland. The London work (supported by the London Arts Board), saw workshops targeted at specific groups of young people: Asian, African/Caribbean, Turkish, the disabled, refugees and asylum seekers. Alongside these, a series of workshops open to anyone under the age of twenty-four was held and some workshops were held in schools. In Northern Ireland (supported by the Arts Council of Northern Ireland) we forged partnerships with community and arts organizations: the Old Museum Arts Centre in Belfast, the Riverside Theatre at the University of Ulster in Coleraine and the Verbal Arts Centre in Derry.

For the first meeting with the young writers during the festival, we provide a one-day workshop during which we aim to encourage them to come up with ideas for development and, most importantly, we aim to foster the energy in those young people to face a blank page and begin their play once we have left. With this in mind, a member of the Young People's Theatre team, together with a professional playwright associated with the Royal Court, will spend a day with the group leading a series of exercises. The structure of the day changes from team to team but the following are some of my favourite exercises:

– We might begin by asking each member of the group to introduce themselves to us and at the same time to tell us three things about themselves, one of which is a lie. The group then decides collectively which thing they think is false and we can make teaching points about the importance in playwriting of a character's credibility and individuality.
– The group divides into pairs and one partner will tell the

other a story of their most embarrassing moment. They
then swap over and the other one will tell the story of
his or her most frightening experience. The partners
then decide whether they will tell their own story or that
of the other person. The stories are then retold to the
whole group with each partner re-telling the story as his
or her own. The group is then asked to comment on
whether they think the story belongs to the teller or their
partner. The point of this exercise is to bring out the
writer's commitment to characterization, including
vocabulary, and to show how useful personal experience
can be to a writer and how important specific detail is in
fleshing out character. (It is also at this stage that the
professional playwright might be seen frantically
scribbling down some of the tales revealed by the group
for future use.)
Staying with characterization, each member of the
group is asked to think carefully about someone that
they know. The person may be a friend, a relative, a
colleague – it doesn't matter. Once they have this person
clearly in mind, they are asked to spend ten minutes or
so writing down sentences and phrases that this person
might use. At this stage, we are not looking for a fully
formed scene, simply a series of unconnected utterances.
The group then comes together and the writers are
asked to read out their list of phrases. The rest of the
group then pass comment or ask questions about the
character depicted: What sex are they? How old are
they? What do we know about their character? etc. This
exercise reinforces the importance of idiom and
language and requires the embryonic writers to avoid
generalization and concentrate on individual speech
patterns (this was the starting point for *The Knocky*).
Other exercises may introduce the importance of a
subtext or of locating a scene – *Essex Girls* was triggered
by the latter. Perhaps the most important thing that we

stress in a playwriting workshop is that drawing on personal experience or knowledge is a good way to approach writing for the theatre and so we encourage the writer to research and to have confidence in the world of their play.

Two months or so after the first workshop, having added a director and actors to the team, we run a second during which we put some of the writing generated by the group 'on its feet', that is to say, exploring the playwright's intentions in a practical way. This way we can demonstrate the strengths and weaknesses of particular pieces of work and at the same time make more generalized teaching points. Obviously there are no rules as to how to write a play any more than there are for any other art form. However, it is often worthwhile to stress how different stage time is to television time, for example, or to explore how an understanding of subtext may influence dialogue within a scene. We also stress the importance of elements involved in the making of a piece of theatre: design, sound, lighting, the effect of an audience. Everyone who has written a piece for this stage of the festival will also receive a one-to-one tutorial where their work is discussed in more detail. In the gaps between and after the workshops run by the Royal Court, staff at the local centres will provide their own invaluable developmental support.

When the drafts of plays arrive at the Royal Court, a panel of playwrights, directors and other experts gather once a week to discuss the plays submitted. As a result of this, a number of writers are invited to spend an intensive and exhilarating weekend at the Royal Court further developing their work – again with actors, directors and writers. After this we are ready to programme the festival.

The festival itself consists of full productions of some of the plays we have received from young people as well as rehearsed readings, platform performances and many other events. Not all the plays featured in the last festival are published in this volume. Jeanne-Anne Craig (then aged 10) and Thomas McLaughlin (11), both from Derry, had their work produced. So did Hayley Daniel (15), who had attended the festival workshops in Bristol two years before and who, we were delighted to discover, had continued her writing to produce the play *Looking for Home*. We also showcase work written by members of the Young People's Theatre Writers' Group, which is performed by members of the Youth Theatre. Work by other young writers is produced at the Royal Court during the festival, in the form of readings or staged extracts in the bars, the foyer and, this year, recorded dialogue in the lavatories.

The Royal Court/Marks & Spencer Young Writers' Festival continues to play a unique and crucial role as part of the UK's cultural life. The young people participating in the festival gain insights into the making of theatre, passed on by those at the top of their profession, and are encouraged to see the medium as one through which to explore their ideas and preoccupations. Some of these responses to the world are produced at the world's most famous 'new writing' theatre.

I hope that you enjoy the plays in this volume of *Coming on Strong*. If you are between sixteen and twenty-five and are able to come to our writers workshops I hope that this has inspired you to join the Young People's Theatre. Alternatively, if you are not yet twenty-four, festival workshops may be taking place near you.

Dominic Tickell
Director, Royal Court Young People's Theatre
June 1995

Acknowledgements

To our most enlightened sponsors, Marks & Spencer, and in particular to Elizabeth Callender, our grateful thanks for the continuing support given to the Royal Court Young Writers' Festival.

Thanks to all the playwrights, directors and workshop leaders who have supported the work of the Young People's Theatre and Festival.

These include April de Angelis, Sharman Macdonald, Clare McIntyre, Winsome Pinnock, Burt Caesar, Stephen Jeffreys, Elyse Dodgson, Robin Hooper, Max Stafford-Clark, Martin Crimp, Ewan Marshall, Janet Steel, Parv Bancil, Shamim Azad, Stephen Daldry, Mary Peate, Philip Osment, Meera Syal, 'Biyi Bandele-Thomas, Andrew Alty, Philip Howard, Tamsin Oglesby, Jane Collins, Brian Stirner, Simon Magill, Heremy Herrin, Guy Chapman, Bo Barton, Chris Samuels, to all of the professional actors who have worked with us to develop writing by young people and to the indefatigable staff of the Young People's Theatre: Roxana Silbert, Ollie Animashawun and Celine Corbin.

A very special thank you to all the members of the Youth Theatre and the other young people with whom we have worked in the past.

PEACHES

Nick Grosso

Characters

Cherry, Rugby
Nikki, South London
Emma, South London
Frank, North London
Brian, Rugby
Johnny, North London
Barmaid
Pete, North London
Pippa, West London
Rob, North London
Shop Assistant, Wolverhampton
Apart from Brian and the shop assistant all the characters
are in their early to early-mid twenties.

Part One
Nightclub, Leeds: Frank, Nikki, Cherry and Emma
Ford Escort van, M1 southbound: Frank and Emma
Ford Sierra, M1 northbound: Frank and Cherry
Country house, Rugby: Frank, Cherry and Brian
Heroes of Alma, NW8: Frank and Johnny

Part Two
Bull and Bush, NW3: Frank, Johnny and barmaid
Flat 89a, NW5: Frank, Johnny and Pete
Crockers Folly, NW8: Frank and Pippa
VW Polo, NW6: Frank and Rob
Clothes shop, NW1: Frank and shop assistant

Peaches was first performed at the Royal Court Theatre Upstairs in association with the Royal National Theatre Studio on 10 November 1994 with the following cast:

Cherry Holly Aird
Nikki/Shop assistant/Barmaid Kate Ashfield
Brian/Rob/Pete Matt Bardock
Frank Ben Chaplin
Emma/Pippa Kate Hardie
Johnny Ian Kirby

Director James Macdonald
Designer David Roger

Part One

SCENE ONE

Leeds. Nightclub. Dance music in the background.
Cherry, **Nikki** *and* **Emma** *are standing at the bar.* **Frank**
walks on.

Frank Hello girls, talking about me again?

Nikki Yeah petal, we just can't stop thinking about ya.

Frank I can imagine, I have the same problem.

> *They laugh. Cherry is leaning across the bar holding a tenner waiting to be served.*

You buying the beers dear?

Cherry As usual.

Frank Good girl.

Nikki Where you been honey?

Frank Downstairs, looking.

Nikki Oh yeah?

Frank Yeah . . . why, what you saying?

Nikki Nothing.

> *Cherry hands Nikki and Emma a can of Red Stripe.*

Thanks petal.

> *Nikki and Emma walk off. Cherry hands Frank a can of Red Stripe.*

Frank Cheers Cherry.

Cherry Frank, if I tell you a secret do you promise you won't tell anyone?

Frank What is it?

Cherry Do you promise?

Frank Yeah course I do.

Cherry You gotta swear you won't tell a soul.

Frank I just told ya, what is it?

Cherry You gotta swear!

Frank Okay, for Christ's sake I swear.

Cherry No I can't tell you.

Frank Why not?

Cherry I can't tell you.

Frank Come on girl that ain't fair.

Cherry It's a *really really* big secret . . .

Frank Yeah I know, you already said.

Pause.

Cherry I'm only telling you b/cos I'm drunk.

Frank Just tell me will ya!

Pause.

Cherry I've got the biggest crush on you.

Pause.

Frank You're joking!

Cherry No.

Frank Since when?

Cherry Since the First Year.

Frank You're joking?

Cherry No.

Pause.

Frank You're joking?

Cherry Look I shouldn't have told you, I'm sorry – I'm really embarrassed now.

Frank That's okay, don't worry about it.

Cherry No look – just pretend I never told you.

Frank I can't do that . . . how come you say it now anyhow, I mean after three years?

Cherry I just thought, we won't see each other again and . . . look let's just forget I said it, I feel like such a fool.

Frank Don't worry – I'm used to it, it happens all the time.

Cherry Yeah, right.

Frank Serious (*laughs*). Anyhow, how come you never showed me, I thought you were pretty up front with guys?

Cherry What do you mean!?

Frank I mean . . . just . . . you know . . . you're usually pretty up front.

Cherry I'm not sure what you mean!?

Frank I don't mean anything – I just mean, you know . . . (*laughs*).

Cherry Well . . . I knew you had a girlfriend. I didn't want to confuse you. After everything with Justin I knew I couldn't get involved.

Pause.

Frank It's funny – I mean I always thought, sometimes you acted a bit cold.

Cherry Cold?

Frank Yeah you know, I mean . . . just . . . like . . . you know . . .

Cherry No I wasn't cold, maybe I was just being careful . . . when we used to go out and talk, I thought maybe something would happen – seeing you and Chrissie together . . . it brought it all home . . . I showed you to my mum . . .

Frank Your mum!

Cherry I told her all about you.

Frank I thought it was meant to be a secret.

Cherry I tell my mum everything.

Frank What did she say?

Cherry She told me to steer clear.

Frank Why?

Cherry B/cos of Chrissie.

Pause.

Frank Did she like me?

Cherry My mum?

Frank Yeah, you know – did she think I was sexy?

Cherry Yeah, right – she wanted your phone number.

They laugh.

Frank Have you told anyone else?

8

Cherry No no-one, I didn't want it to get out. I told Sophie once – she was so drunk I doubt she remembers.

Nikki walks on. Pause. Frank walks off.

Nikki Alright chick. What's up?

Cherry I can't believe it . . .

Nikki Why what happened? What you been saying?

Cherry I can't believe what I've just done – I've made such a fool of myself.

Nikki You didn't tell him you . . . you haven't have you? Oh no! You told him! Oh no! I can't believe you did that!

Cherry nods her head painfully.

(*shrieks*) Oh no . . . chicken! I can't believe you did that! *Shit*. What did he say?

Cherry I feel like such a fool.

Nikki Oh no chicken. What did he say, what did *you* say?

Cherry I just told him I fancied him.

Nikki What! Just like that?

Cherry I asked him if he could keep a secret and then I told him.

Nikki Oh no! Oh chicken . . . what did he say?

Cherry He just said something about my mum, he wanted her phone number . . . he called me a tart, I think, I don't know, he didn't really say anything . . . oh no, I can't believe I just did that!

Nikki hugs Cherry.

Nikki Aah chicken, don't worry petal . . . it's probably for

9

the best hey. *Christ*, I can't believe you did that. You're so brave! I could never do something like that . . . shit, you're so brave . . . he called you a tart!?

They cackle with laughter. Emma walks on.

Emma What's up with you two?

Cherry I just told Frank I fancy him.

Emma You didn't! Oh Cherry you silly cow! What did he say?

Cherry He called me a cheap whore.

Emma You're joking!

Cherry He asked for my mum's phone number.

Emma No! You're joking! The cheeky swine . . . you're joking!

Cherry No.

Emma The dirty swine . . . mind you she's quite attractive your mum – her bits are still in all the right places.

They laugh.

I noticed Duncan looking at her.

Cherry You're joking!

Emma Straight up, and his girlfriend was there. She wears too much foundation. Have you seen her?

Cherry I know.

Emma She was eyeing up my Danny as well, the lecherous cow. I tell ya Cherry, if she'd tried to pull a stunt I'd have scratched her eyes out no messing. I don't care who was there.

They laugh.

Did Frank really say that? You're kidding! The cheeky swine, imagine saying that! Since when have you liked him? I never knew you liked him. You never told me.

Cherry I've always liked him. Big time.

Emma You never told me . . . you never told me . . .

They laugh. Frank walks on. Cherry and Emma run off laughing.

Frank What they laughing at?

Nikki I don't know.

Frank What's up?

Nikki Nothing.

Frank What you been saying . . . what she been saying?

Nikki Who?

Frank Cherry . . . Nikki?

Nikki She just said what she told you.

Frank I like that . . .

Nikki I already knew.

Frank How come?

Nikki I asked her two weeks ago.

Frank How come?

Nikki I could tell, the way she acted with you.

Frank Like what?

Nikki Just the way she behaved.

Frank It's funny – I never woulda guessed.

Nikki Well . . . a woman knows these things honey.

Frank Yeah . . .?

Nikki nods her head.

I suppose so.

SCENE TWO

M1 Southbound. Ford Escort Van. Cassette in the background. Frank is driving, Emma is in the passenger seat.

Emma Did you know Micky Bainbridge?

Frank Mister heart-throb?

Emma You sound jealous.

Frank Jealous? Why should I be jealous?

Emma I just thought, the way you said it.

Frank I got no problem with heart throbs – the way I see it some guys are heart throbs some guys ain't. I'm one of the lucky ones. Ain't no big deal.

Emma If you say so . . . I must admit he was kinda smooth.

Frank Yeah yeah. So is Guinness.

Emma If you'd rather not talk about it . . .

Frank Nah, I love Micky Bainbridge . . . what about him anyway?

Emma No let's just leave it.

Frank No – I wanna know.

Emma It ain't nothing. Just that I used to know him that's all.

Frank Oh yeah?

Emma Not like that! We just hung out together for a while.

Frank Oh yeah?

Emma We were just friends.

Pause.

Frank So what was he like?

Emma He was a walking hard-on, a prick on legs. I swear he thought the whole world fancied him.

Frank So how come you hung out with him?

Emma Well when he got back from LA he didn't have a place and we kinda got friendly one night and I said he could crash at mine . . .

Frank Oh yeah?

Emma Yeah.

Frank That was nice of you.

Pause.

Emma Anyway we stayed up most of the night just talking, it was really cool . . . we ended up sleeping in my bed – but nothing happened I swear – anyway he ended up staying two months.

Frank Two months!

Emma Yeah – on the sofa of course. The bastard wouldn't leave. I swear right he fucking sponged off me the whole fucking time – never once bought any food or did any cleaning. I fucking had to clean up after him!

Frank You're joking!

Emma No. He used to bring that Nigel round and they'd stay up all night popping acid and playing video games, laughing as well so you couldn't sleep. He used to eat my toast in the morning, my milk, never bought his own shampoo or anything. And then there were the girls – he used to bring these girls round, fuck knows where he picked them up from, some of them – and I'm not joking right – some of them weren't even sixteen.

Frank You're joking!

Emma No. I'm not joking. Not even sixteen. I used to wake up in the morning and see these young tarts lounging about in their knickers. Using *my* bathroom! I swear. And they never said a word. Sometimes I felt like making them a packed lunch to take to school.

  They laugh.

Frank That musta been hard for you to take.

Emma It was.

  Emma looks at Frank reproachfully.

What do you mean, hard for me to take?

Frank I mean . . . how come you let it go anyhow?

Emma I didn't – I dropped a thousand fucking hints but the bastard was so thick skinned. He thought the sun shone out of his hole.

  Pause.

Frank You see, that wouldn't happen with me . . .

Emma Uh . . .?

Frank If I was living with you . . .

Emma What?

Frank Just say for instance I was staying at yours for two weeks, or ten days say – on the sofa – you wouldn't have those problems . . .

Emma What you talking about?

Frank I'm just saying you'd get no grief – I'd buy my own toast, my own shampoo, everything. I'd make breakfast in the morning, I'd bring it up to ya, I'd tickle your pyjamas – there'd be no-one else, just the two of us . . .

Emma Dirty swine . . .

They laugh.

Listen to this, one morning right, I'm making breakfast and he comes into the kitchen and just sits down, without saying nothing, just sits down, and watches me, so I carry on with whatever I'm doing and after a while he says 'you know Emma, you've got a really fat arse' – just like that.

Frank You're joking!

Emma No, he goes 'you've got a *really* fat arse.'

Frank What did you say?

Emma I wanted to smack him.

Frank Did he really say that!?

Emma I swear!

Frank He musta been fooling around.

Emma He weren't. He wanted it to sound like he was, you know, but you could tell by the way he said it . . . I mean it didn't bother me cos I know my arse ain't fat . . .

Frank Your arse is fine.

Emma Thanks . . . but all the same it upset me. I kept looking at it in the mirror . . . once we went shopping right, and I bought these pair of green jeans, really nice they were, cost me forty quid, anyway, just as I'd paid for them and we're walking out the shop he says 'you look really fat in those jeans' . . .

Frank No!

Emma He goes 'you look *really* fat in those jeans' – just as we've left the shop and we're walking up the road. I'd spent about an hour trying on a million different pairs and he'd not said nothing. Not a fucking word. Then soon as I've forked out for them he says that. I could have belted him.

Frank You shoulda.

Emma Soon as I got home I felt like taking them back. Then I thought that was stupid.

Frank I've never seen you in green jeans.

Emma That's cos I've never fucking worn them.

   Pause. Emma looks at Frank coyly.

Anyway, what did Cherry say to you last night?

   Pause.

Frank You know what she said.

Emma She's a nice girl, Cherry.

Frank Yeah. I suppose so . . . he's having a scene with Cindy.

Emma Micky? I know.

Frank She's alright is Cindy.

Emma Dya like her?

Frank She's alright.

16

Emma What's so great about her?

Frank Nothing. I just said she's alright.

Pause.

Emma She's got funny legs.

SCENE THREE

M1 northbound. Ford Sierra. Cherry is driving, Frank is in the passenger seat.

Frank What are those marks on your neck, Cherry?

They laugh.

Cherry My ex-boyfriend . . .

Frank Oh yeah? Which one?

Cherry Mark.

Frank The guy from Coventry?

Cherry Yeah.

Frank Well! He likes you!

They laugh.

What happened?

Cherry I met him in the pub on Saturday and we got chatting – we got absolutely hammered and . . . he ended up coming back to my sister's.

Frank Oh yeah?

Cherry It was terrible . . .

Frank Why?

Cherry Well . . . he had to shoot off really early so his girlfriend wouldn't find out. About six in the morning . . . it was really awful, it just brought back everything with Justin . . .

Frank Shit.

Cherry Yeah. My mum was really livid.

Frank Your mum!

Cherry I went back and told her everything.

Frank Did you give her my number by the way?

Cherry Yeah, right. She'll phone you next Tuesday.

They laugh.

Frank Why was she angry?

Cherry She tells me not to regress – she thinks it's bad for me.

Frank She's probably right.

Cherry I know. My sister said the same.

Frank Which one?

Cherry Lucy.

Frank Which one's she?

Cherry My younger one.

Frank She the one I saw at Tesco's?

Cherry Yeah.

Frank She's a looker isn't she?

Cherry Yeah, she's beautiful . . . she's got a naturally good figure – her legs just go on for ever, lucky thing.

Frank Yeah, she's a fucking peach . . . how old is she?

Cherry Fourteen.

Frank Fourteen! Shit! She looks about twenty-five!

Cherry She doesn't.

Frank Shit. Fourteen.

Cherry Too young for you is she? Maybe in a few years . . .

Frank Too young for me. Too old for Micky Bainbridge.

Cherry What!

Frank Just something I heard.

Cherry From Emma?

They look at each other and laugh.

Frank So Lucy's not so keen on Mark?

Cherry Not really.

Frank Good.

Cherry What's good about it?

Frank shrugs his shoulders.

Frank So she gives you advice does she? Your fourteen year old sister!

Cherry I know! It's a joke isn't it, tells you what kinda state I'm in . . . she's the only reason I can stick Rugby.

Frank Ain't you got friends there?

Cherry Not really, most of my friends live in Coventry, and that's half an hour drive. Usually I ain't got the car.

Frank Why not?

Cherry It's my sister's.

Frank Which one?

Cherry Michelle – the one who's on holiday.

Pause.

Frank So you've got her house *and* her car?

Cherry Yeah, till she gets back.

Pause.

Frank When's that?

Cherry Not till next week.

Pause.

Frank (*under his breath*) Shit . . . (*He pulls out a cigarette.*)

Cherry What?

Frank I see . . . (*He lights the cigarette.*)

Cherry Then I go back to my mum's.

Frank What's that like?

Cherry It's alright – be better if I had my own room.

Frank Where dya sleep then?

Cherry In Lucy's room – she sleeps on the floor.

Frank What, you sleep in her bed and she sleeps on the floor? And she puts up with that?

Cherry She insists on it – I tell her not to be so silly but she won't listen. She likes it. She loves sharing with me – she keeps me up most nights talking. Sometimes we hardly get any sleep.

Frank What dya talk about?

Cherry I tell her about guys mostly and she gives me all the gossip from school.

Frank I bet she's got a few fans.

Cherry Not really.

Frank She's gonna break a few hearts.

Cherry There was this one guy, from the next town, he used to get the same bus as her in the morning.

Frank What happened?

Cherry He was eighteen. They caught the same bus for two years but never spoke. One day he goes up to her and says he's really in love with her – how she's really pretty and every morning he sits at the back of the bus just so he can look at her, and how he's really upset when she gets off and how he watches her from the window. It was really sweet. He asked her out.

Frank What did she say?

Cherry She told him she'd think about it. She came home and asked mum if it was alright, they had this really long talk about it and mum said it was okay so long as she was back by ten. Lucy was really excited.

Frank So what happened?

Cherry Well they arranged to go to the pictures that Friday. Lucy was really nervous, I'd never seen her so nervous – on Friday she came back from school and just *camped* in front of the mirror, she tried on everything she had, all my clothes, all my sister's clothes, all my mum's clothes – we all helped her. In the end she got so nervous, it was awful, she decided she couldn't go through with it – she rang him up about seven and told him.

Frank What did she say?

Cherry She was so cool – I was so impressed. She handled it much better than I could. She just said she really liked him and she was really flattered and everything but she felt she was too young for him.

Frank How did he take it?

Cherry He was really cool. He said he understood – he said he was gonna take another bus in the morning so they wouldn't get embarrassed.

Frank Fucking hell.

Cherry Yeah. Lucy was really upset. He sent her a letter a week later saying all these sweet things, how he thought about her all the time . . . he said he hoped they'd meet again one day, when she's older, and she'd let him take her out. He asked her to send him a picture of her so he'd always have something to look at.

Frank He sounds like a case.

Cherry He was really sweet. I took a picture of Lucy in the garden – we made her really beautiful.

Frank Shit.

Cherry It was so sweet . . .

Pause. Frank chuckles to himself.

Frank That reminds me of my brother.

Cherry What?

Frank Some thing *exactly*. This girl from Bethnal Green – Melinda or Belinda or something. He saw her in the street. Said she was the living peach.

Cherry So what happened?

Frank He took her to the market and bought her a necklace . . .

Cherry Aah . . .

Frank And lunch and a taxi back to hers . . .

Pause.

Cherry And?

Frank Nothing. They get out the cab, walk to the door, she pecks him on the cheek and thanks him for a pleasant afternoon. A pleasant afternoon!? He'd spent the best part of a ton!

Cherry Frank . . .?

Frank Talk about being short changed. (*He shakes his head ruefully.*) Belinda she was called . . . they met on Three Colts Lane.

Cherry Frank, are you taking the piss?

Frank I know – unbelievable innit.

SCENE FOUR

Rugby. Country house. Tina Turner in the background. Cherry is in the kitchen offstage making dinner. Frank is in the room adjacent, onstage, slouched on the sofa watching TV. Their shoes are off.

Cherry Do you like sprouts . . .? Frank!

Frank Uh . . . What?

Cherry Do you like sprouts?

Frank They're alright.

Cherry sighs.

Cherry?

Cherry appears inside the doorway.

Cherry What?

Frank Is there any videos?

Cherry Videos? Yeah. They're right there. (*She disappears.*)

Frank Any without Tina Turner?

Cherry I think there's an Eric Clapton there somewhere.

Pause.

Frank (*under his breath*) Great.

Pause.

Cherry I'll be ready in a minute . . . what would you like to drink?

Frank What have you got?

Cherry walks on holding a tray with two plates. She hands one to Frank.

Wicked.

Cherry Careful, it's hot.

Frank puts the plate on his lap. Cherry sits down beside him and puts her plate on her lap. Frank takes a mouthful.

Frank Shit! It's hot!

Cherry I told you!

Frank For fuck's sake!

Pause.

Cherry Do you like it?

Frank Mmmm it's delicious . . . what's in it?

Cherry Just vegetables.

Frank Vegetables! You mean there's no meat in it!?

Cherry No.

Frank That's amazing! It tastes delicious . . . you sure it ain't got a bit of chicken?

Cherry Quite sure.

Frank A little bit of bacon?

Cherry Why don't you believe me Frank?

Frank That's amazing – it tastes delicious.

Pause.

Cherry I don't eat meat.

Frank What?

Cherry I don't eat meat. I'm a vegetarian.

Frank Shit . . . I never knew that . . . a vegetarian . . . shit.

Frank takes another mouthful.

Cherry What would you like to drink? There's beer, wine, cider . . .

Frank I'm alright with my tea.

Cherry Sure?

Frank Yeah.

Cherry It's not like you to turn down a drink.

Frank I'm alright with my tea.

Pause. Cherry gets up and walks off. She returns with a glass in her hand. She sits down and takes a sip.

What's that?

Cherry Cider.

Pause.

25

Frank I never knew you liked cider.

Cherry My sister's boyfriend brews it . . .

Frank What, you mean he brews his own cider?

Cherry That's what I just said.

Frank Shit. Where does he do that?

Cherry In the shed. There's tons of it.

Frank Shit – that's a good idea. How does he do that?

Cherry I don't know – he's always done it.

Frank Shit . . . that's a good idea. And you say there's tons of it?

Cherry Yeah. Barrels full. Do you want some?

Frank No, I'm alright with my tea . . . what's it like?

Cherry It's nice. Try some.

Frank Maybe later . . . is it strong?

Cherry It's lethal. Two pints and you can't pick yourself off the floor.

Frank Shit.

Cherry It's great.

Pause.

Frank Shit . . . so how old's your sister's boyfriend then?

Cherry Barry . . .? About twenty-nine.

Pause.

Frank Twenty-nine.

Someone is heard entering the house. The front door slams.

Who the fuck's that?

Cherry I don't know. It might be my mum . . .

Frank *Your mum!*

Cherry Or Lucy I suppose.

Frank *Lucy?*

Cherry You know – my little sister.

Frank *Shit.*

Frank straightens his hair and composes himself. The fridge is heard being opened and closed. **Brian** *appears holding a four-pack of beer. He stands inside the doorway.*

Brian Hello Cherry dear.

Cherry gets up to greet Brian.

Cherry Brian! Hi! How are you?

Brian Not too bad, you know. I saw Michelle's motor outside, for a moment there I thought they'd got back – I thought 'shit, I'm up the creek – Barry's gonna kill me.'

Cherry Why? What have you done?

Brian I'm supposed to mow the lawn and do a few things you see, I thought 'shit, I'm up the creek!'

Cherry They don't get back till Tuesday.

Brian Tuesday is it? That's good . . . aye, that's what I thought.

Cherry Brian, this is a friend of mine from Leeds, Frank.

Brian walks over to shake Frank's hand.

Brian Pleased to meet you Frank.

Frank Nice to meet you.

Brian From Leeds you say?

Frank That's right.

Pause.

Brian Well . . . listen Cherry, I'm off, Sarah's waiting for me – I thought I'd just pop in and grab a beer, you know – don't say nothing to Barry . . .

They laugh.

He won't miss it. I'll see ya, ta-ra.

Cherry See ya Brian.

Brian walks off and leaves the house. Cherry walks towards Frank and kneels on the floor. Pause.

Frank Who was that?

Cherry Brian – Barry's best mate.

Frank I see . . . did you see the look on his face?

Cherry No – what look?

Frank The way he looked at me.

Cherry No.

Frank Shit.

Cherry What's the matter?

Frank Listen Cherry, where's the bedroom?

Cherry The bedroom? What for?

Frank You know what for.

Cherry I'm sorry?

Pause.

Frank Look, let's just face things – we're in the country for Christ's sake.

Cherry So?

Frank So, we're a million miles from anything, we've got the place all to ourselves . . . no-one's gonna believe we came down here just to watch videos.

Cherry What do you mean?

Frank You know what I mean – everyone thinks we're at it. Everyone thinks we're at it, we might as well do it. That Brian, did you see his face? You could tell what he was thinking – Nikki, Emma, Sophie, they all think we're at it. And fuck knows who else . . .

Cherry No-one thinks anything.

Frank Come on Cherry, did you see his face . . .?

Cherry So that's why you want to do it is it? B/cos it's expected of you?

Frank What?

Cherry B/cos everyone thinks we're 'at it' – that's reason enough is it?

Frank Come on Cherry . . . you know what this is . . .

Cherry What *what* is?

Frank This! Vegetable pie, cider in the shed . . .

Cherry We've been friends for three years Frank, and we hardly know each other.

Frank Of course we know each other.

Cherry You never knew I was a vegetarian.

Frank How long have you been a vegetarian?

Cherry Six years.

Pause.

Frank Just cos someone's a vegetarian don't mean you don't know them.

Cherry I thought we could get to know each other better . . . anyway, what about Chrissie?

Frank Even if we don't do it they'll still think we did it . . .

Cherry So?

Frank So we might as well do it.

Cherry It's not what I want.

Frank What do you want?

Cherry I don't want to go to bed for you to run straight back to Chrissie.

Frank This ain't about Chrissie, Cherry. It's about you and me . . .

Cherry I don't want to be taken for a ride Frank. I'm tired of all that.

Frank It won't be like *that*.

Cherry What will it be like?

Frank I don't know . . . shit . . . you started all this.

SCENE FIVE

NW8. Heroes of Alma pub. Pints of lager. Frank and **Johnny** *are sitting at a table.*

Frank So we end up going back to Rugby, back to her

sister's. This beautiful little country house, Tina Turner CDs and shit.

They laugh.

I love those country houses, everything is so neat and made of wood, and frilly bows. Play better golf videos.

They laugh.

Everything smells of country, dya know what I mean? And it's cold. It don't matter how hot it is, it's always fucking cold. Cold and damp. And dark. Shit, I love the country.

Johnny Yeah, I love the fucking country.

Frank And there ain't no shops for miles, not even a newsagents, they're all in town – fifty miles down the fucking road. I mean what happens if you run out of milk?

Johnny You grab a cow.

Frank But imagine Johnny! You're having a smoke and you run outa Rizlas – you gotta drive fifty fucking miles just for some skins! You want a Kit-Kat or something. A can of Coke. A packet of fags! I mean what the fuck do you do?

Johnny Yeah. I love the country.

Pause.

Frank What if you need some stamps?

Johnny Some taramasalata.

Frank Your car breaks down?

Johnny You ain't got a car.

Frank Exactly! You gotta *walk* fifty fucking miles down a narrow country road with no pavement, tractors keep running you over, ducks keep biting your legs, snakes and all sorts, you're shivering your balls off and it's raining, you're walking barefoot in the gravel, cow pats everywhere . . . stray bits of glass.

Johnny You get struck by lightning!

Frank You pop off to the shops and you're not seen again, no one thinks it funny. 'You seen Frank lately?' – 'Oh he just popped out to the shops *five* days ago!' Meanwhile your body's decomposing . . .

Johnny Wild dogs are eating your kidneys . . . there must be local shops.

Frank All there is is farms – horseshit and farms. All they sell is eggs and cheese!

Johnny What about fish fingers?

Frank All they sell is fucking yogurt. *Natural* yogurt! It tastes like horseshit! You ask for a packet of wine gums they think you're from another planet! They phone up the sheriff and tell him a Martian's on the loose! They put you in a cage and charge folk five shillings to see you. They send you to the knacker's yard and feed you to the pigs! They make yogurt out of you and sell it to the locals. They call it Martian-flavour yogurt. I swear they're all fucking off it! You ask for some wine gums, they think you're doolally – it's like that book, 1974!

Johnny 1984.

Frank Yeah. 1984. Only now it's called 1994 in the fucking sticks!

Pause.

Johnny So what about this girl Cherry?

Frank She's a fucking peach – she takes me back to her sister's and starts making cups of tea, meanwhile I'm parked on the sofa with the remote control, watching Tina Turner in concert. Nick Faldo showing you where to put your knees.

They laugh.

Then she starts on dinner. She makes the most pristine food you've ever seen, cauliflower and spuds and sprouts, steak and kidney pie Johnny . . .

Johnny Shit.

Frank I thought I'd gone to heaven. Glass of cider, not the shit you get down here, proper country cider from the country.

Johnny Full of country goodness.

Frank That's right – it almost tasted like yogurt. My head started spinning.

Johnny Sounds good.

Frank Man I thought I was gonna die! Her brother-in-law brewed the stuff in his shed, next to his combine harvester. Gallons and gallons of the stuff! I thought to myself 'shit Frank you could really live like this.' I mean, nice house in the country, full of country air, patchwork quilts, Tina Turner videos, as much cider as you can down . . . I thought 'shit, I could *really* live like this!'

Johnny So why don't you?

Frank I thought about it . . . we didn't have anything to talk about, I kept looking round in case her mum showed up.

Johnny Her mum!?

Frank Yeah her mum's a real dish – she's got the hots for me too. She's calling me on Tuesday. Pity it ain't her sister.

Johnny Her *mum's* sister!

Frank No! Cherry's. She's got this sister you wouldn't believe! She looks like a fucking peach.

Johnny Yeah? How old?

Frank Sixteen . . . fourteen.

They laugh.

Yeah, fourteen going on twenty-five. She's got this long golden brown hair – it goes down to about her knees. And it glistens. In sunlight it shines as well as glistens. And it just sways under the sky . . . she's called Lucille – if you're ever in Rugby look out for her. She takes the bus every morning.

Johnny What? She takes the bus every morning? In Rugby?

Frank Yeah. She's called Lucille . . . I ain't met her mum's sister. I'm not sure she's got one – I'll have to find out.

Long pause.

Johnny Frank, dya know Raymond Chandler?

Frank Yeah . . . didn't he play for Fulham?

Johnny No, that was Danny Blanchflower. Raymond Chandler you fool, the writer!

Frank Oh! That Raymond Chandler! Yeah . . . what about him?

Johnny He wrote all those private eye stories – you know, the ones with Bogart.

Frank I love that shit.

Johnny Yeah. Anyway, in the long goodbye he writes this thing – he's sitting in his office, high in the sky, drinking a Scotch . . .

Frank Wicked.

Johnny Yeah. Only there they don't drink Scotch, they drink bourbon.

Frank Wicked.

Johnny He's looking out his window saying what he sees – the dirt on the streets, the oil in the gutters, the smoke in the air, the tramps, the booze, the whores, the thieves, the sleaze, the sweat . . .

Frank The noise.

Johnny Yeah, the noise. All the shit that exists basically. He says it like it's a real shithole. Then he says 'yeah – the city's a mess, give me the city any time.'

Pause.

Frank He says that?

Johnny Yeah.

Both That's fucking cool.

Frank I love Chandler – he knows how to say things. He obviously knew Rugby.

Johnny Probably.

Frank And they made a film of that? With Humphrey?

Johnny Yeah.

Frank Shit. We gotta see it. Dya think it's on at the flicks?

Johnny Don't be stupid.

Frank Shit. They should show those films . . .

Pause.

Johnny So what happened with Cherry?

Frank I tell ya, sometimes *I* feel like Bogart – one guy and 57 babes. The way I see it, there's only one of you, and about six million babes in this town – so whichever way you look you're outnumbered. So you better get to work. There's no point being old and saying you lived a little, talking about the war – you gotta talk about *babes* when you're old, tell your grandkids all about it. Fuck the fucking war!

Johnny So what happened after dinner?

Frank I kept waiting for her sister to show, I kept thinking of that long golden hair. In the end I got the train home.

Johnny What did Cherry say?

Frank She was sweet. We kissed at the station. We sorted everything out, sorta . . . and I'm on the train, riding home, and I'm thinking what a good guy I am – I mean there I was with this sexy gal, country house all to ourselves, a million miles from anyone, and she's offering it to me on a plate. And I don't do nothing. And I'm paying for my ticket, all alone, and I'm thinking 'shit you're a fucking saint' . . . but the thing is, I didn't feel good about it. I didn't feel good at all – I felt like a fucking fool. All I could think of were her great big bamboolas.

They laugh.

I thought 'where's the fun in being good – where's the perks, where's the glory?' No-one shakes your hand or gives you a medal. There's no fucking glory.

Part Two

SCENE ONE

NW3. Bull and Bush pub. Pints of lager and whisky chasers. Frank and Johnny are sitting at a table.

Frank Did I tell ya I'm seeing Pippa on Monday?

Johnny You're kidding!

Frank No.

Johnny Where?

Frank The Crocks.

Johnny How come?

Frank She called me last night and said she wanted to see me.

Johnny And you know what that means. (*His eyebrows bounce up and down.*)

Frank It don't mean nothing – she just wants to talk.

Johnny That's what she says.

Frank She just wants to talk – that's all.

Johnny Frank, don't you get anything? She says she just wants to talk but that's just so she can get you down there. After a few rum and Cokes you won't be talking – you'll be back at hers getting fresh on the carpet.

Frank This time it ain't like that – besides she don't drink rum she drinks vodka.

Johnny How come she wants to talk to you anyway?

37

Frank She misses me that's all. I can understand that – I'm a very missable guy.

Johnny Miserable?

Frank *Missable*.

Johnny So all of a sudden she decides she's missing you?

Frank It ain't all of a sudden Johnny – it's probably been building up, till she has to see me just to keep herself sane. I mean you don't need a reason to miss someone, you just miss them that's all – ain't no logic behind it! You start thinking about them and wanting them back, the night draws in and you get lonely, you want some company . . .

Johnny Someone to talk to.

Frank Someone to pay you a bit of attention.

Johnny A little affection.

Frank Right.

Johnny Sounds like she misses you bad.

Frank She can't *live* without me basically.

Johnny So she just rings you out the blue . . .?

Frank Well – not exactly . . .

Johnny What dya mean not exactly?

Frank It didn't exactly come out the blue.

Johnny So you're saying you knew she was calling?

Frank Yeah – kinda . . .

Johnny How?

Frank I could sense it.

Johnny So what, you're saying you're psychic?

Frank No I'm not saying I'm psychic – I'm just saying I had a feeling that's all.

Johnny What kinda feeling?

Frank Just a fucking feeling!

Johnny So tell me about this feeling.

Frank What about it?

Johnny Where was it?

Frank What dya mean where was it?

Johnny I mean where was it – was it in your belly, your knees, was it in your dick, was it halfway up your arm . . .?

Frank It was all over!

Johnny All over!

Frank Yeah!

Johnny I ain't stupid Frank.

Frank What you talking about?

Johnny You called her didn't you?

Frank What?

Johnny You called Pippa!

Frank looks at Johnny indignantly.

Frank Let's get one thing straight Johnny – I don't call no-one for nothing, specially some brainless bimbo from Clapham. If people wanna speak to me they know my number, if they don't know my number that's *tough*, if they don't wanna speak to me they're just plain fucking dumb and I don't wanna speak to them. The mountain, my friend, don't move for Mohammed – Mohammed moves for the fucking mountain!

39

Johnny stares into his glass, swirling it around.

Johnny So when did you call her?

Frank Last Friday. Six seventeen precisely.

They laugh.

Johnny And what did you say?

Frank I told her I was miserable.

Johnny Missable?

Frank Miserable.

Johnny What else?

Frank How I liked her, how I cared for her, how I held her in my heart, blah blah blah. I'm a showman with words Johnny – I know just what to say to women.

Johnny And . . .?

Frank She told me to get lost . . . she said I was a self-centred arrogant bastard and hung up.

Johnny You're kidding!

Frank I think she was mixing me up with someone else.

Johnny So what did you do?

Frank I called her again.

Johnny And?

Frank She called me a flake.

Johnny A flake! What, like a Cadbury's Flake?

Frank I know – I thought if she has to insult me the least she could do is call me a Bounty Bar, or something with a bit more bite to it, dya know what I mean?

Johnny Or a Snickers.

Frank Yeah. Or a packet of Rolos.

Johnny Or a Toffee Crisp with 10 per cent extra.

Frank So I asked her 'what dya mean by flake Pippa? Dya mean I'm a little sweetie?'

Johnny Or a Coconut Boost, have you tried them?

Frank She said it meant I was unreliable and inconsistent.

Johnny She said what?

Frank Her exact words – unreliable and inconsistent.

Johnny You shoulda told her – consistency is the refuge of the unimaginative.

Frank What?

Johnny Orson Welles.

Frank Shit. I wish I'd known.

Johnny No – it was Oscar Wilde. I read it in an article about Gazza.

Frank Consistency is the . . . what was it?

Johnny Refuge of the unimaginative.

Frank Refuge of the unimaginative. That's beautiful. I'm gonna tell her that next time – she's gonna hit the fucking floor. I mean if she wants consistency and reliability she should get herself a Volkswagen!

Johnny What else did she say . . .? Frank . . .?

Frank She asked me if I wanted my record back.

Johnny What record?

Frank Just some record I lent her.

Johnny What did you say?

Frank I let her keep it – I said it was something to remember me by. And you know what she said!? You know what she said Johnny!

Johnny What's that?

Frank She said I was vain!

Johnny Nah.

Frank Can you believe it!? After I've just said she can *keep* the record! After I've just given her a gift for fuck's sake! Out the goodness of my precious heart! And she's calling me vain! After I've just given her my Mink Deville . . .

Johnny Mink Deville!? That's not yours! That's mine you bastard! You gave her my Mink Deville!?

Frank What?

Johnny You gave Pippa my Mink Deville!?

Frank Sorry did I say Mink Deville . . .

Johnny Yes you fucking did Frank! Where the fuck is my Mink Deville?

Frank Listen Johnny – I had no choice . . .

Johnny What?

Frank Johnny be reasonable . . .

Johnny Reasonable . . .!

Frank Listen – I'll buy you a drink . . .

Johnny You'll do more than buy me a drink Frank! What the fuck are you doing giving people my records . . .!?

They turn away from each other. A **Barmaid** *walks on and takes their empty pint glasses. Pause.*

42

Frank Can't you see? I didn't *give* it to her, she stole if off me – she asked me on the phone if she could keep it and I was trying to get her to talk to me instead of throwing insults at me every five seconds and she asked for the record and I was trying to get her to come out for a drink and forgive me for being a flake and everything else and she said she wanted it and how much she liked it and I was trapped, *Johnny, I was psychologically trapped*, she was punishing me and I couldn't escape, I knew it was your record but I couldn't say to her 'I'm sorry Pippa, you can't have that record b/cos it's Johnny's and I'm sorry I told you it was mine but I was lying cos I wanted to impress you cos I wanted to get you into bed but here, no problem, you can have my Michael Bolton collection!' I couldn't say that to her could I Johnny!? I mean what's a man supposed to do!? On the one hand he wants to keep the record cos he knows it's his mate's, his very good mate's, *his beloved mate's, Johnny*, who he loves adorably, and on the other he don't wanna appear like a selfish devious bastard who don't give people records just cos they ain't his! I mean I didn't know what to do Johnny, my mind was in a mess, my mouth was dry, my heart was having palpitations – *I thought I was gonna die Johnny!* The paramedics were on standby and I was hallucinating! My back was crippled! I had stomach cramps, *I was chucking up blood* Johnny, I was chucking up blood, and it was green . . .

Johnny Alright! For fuck's sake! Forget about the record . . .

Frank You're a saint Johnny – a real life fucking saint. I'm telling you though, it was bad – I was in a coma and my brain was being amputated . . .!

Frank breaks into a fit of laughter. Johnny laughs, grudgingly.

Johnny That record was the fucking business.

Frank Relax – I'm only joking. I never gave her your Mink Deville. I gave her one of my brother's Duke Ellington's – he's gonna kill me when he finds out.

Johnny looks at Frank wearily.

Johnny You're a fucking wind-up merchant you know that?

Frank nods his head.

So?

Frank What?

Johnny How come you're seeing Pippa?

Frank She rang me last night and said she'd changed her mind. Simple as that.

Johnny looks at Frank knowingly.

It ain't like that, I told ya – we just wanna be friends.

Johnny Friends?

Frank Yeah you know – amigos.

Johnny Amigos?

Frank Amigos. It's Spanish.

Johnny What's got into you?

Frank Nothing. I just like her – I like talking to her . . .

Johnny Frank, be serious.

Frank I am being serious. You see, ever since I've known her we've always played this game . . .

Johnny What, like Monopoly?

Frank Not that kinda game you pillock!

44

Johnny Me and Penny used to play Monopoly – mind you she always cheated . . .

Frank Will you shut up about Monopoly! I'm talking about a mind game . . .

Johnny You mean like chess?

Frank Johnny, forget about Monopoly and chess will ya! I'm not talking about board games, I'm talking about games people play with each other – games that take place in the head . . .

Johnny You mean like cards?

They stare at each other.

Frank We're always scoring points off each other, like it's a great big contest or something . . .

Johnny You mean like Opportunity Knocks?

Frank I'm gonna thump you in a minute!

Johnny (*laughs*) So, you play this game . . .

Frank Yeah. I mean we have a nice time and everything but we never seem to make proper contact – I mean like friends . . .

Johnny Don't you mean amigos?

Frank Anyway, one night we went out for a pizza and Pippa starts talking about her childhood and where she went to school and all her nicknames, I wasn't really listening to be honest, I was too busy checking out this waitress with long black . . . you shoulda seen her Johnny – anyway then she starts talking about her mum and how it's a shame she never remarried and how she's lonely . . .

Johnny So what's her mum's number?

Frank Exactly! Anyway then her eyes swell up and these

tears start trickling down her cheeks and she's crying in the middle of this pizza parlour and everyone's looking at me like I'm a cunt and the waitress comes over and wraps her arms around Pippa and I'm thinking 'shit – I'll have some of that!' So I force a few tears but she didn't wanna know Johnny, she was blind to the depths of my despair . . .!

Johnny Frank, get to the fucking point will ya!

Frank I'm coming to the fucking point! The point is – after that me and Pippa were talking! Proper talking like proper people! Without cracking jokes every minute and without putting the other one down. We opened up with each other. We were honest with each other . . .

Johnny stares at Frank quizzically.

What I'm saying is we broke the barrier.

Johnny So you're gonna get her crying on Monday are ya?

Frank No-one's gonna be crying Johnny . . .

SCENE TWO

NW5. Flat 89A. **Pete** *is in a shirt and boxers ironing another shirt. Frank is lying on the sofa. Johnny is standing.*

Pete I saw Milly yesterday.

Frank and Johnny look at Pete.

Johnny Milly!

Frank Where?

Pete At the bus stop.

Johnny I love Milly.

Frank I love her too.

Johnny Pity she don't love you.

Frank She loves me alright – she just don't know it.

Pete She looked *fresh*.

Johnny Sweet like a puppy.

Frank Yeah – she's a real-life fucking diamond.

Johnny Did you say hello?

Pete Nah. I was driving.

Johnny You fool. You fucked up – you shoulda pulled over.

Frank Yeah, you fucked up. You bad fool.

Johnny Did she see you?

Pete Nah, I was wearing my shades.

Johnny That's it – you fucked up . . . what was she doing?

Pete Standing.

Johnny With who?

Pete On her own.

Frank and Johnny glance at each other.

Both *Safe*.

Johnny Where was this?

Pete At a bus stop.

Johnny *What bus stop?*

Pete I don't know – a bus stop – they all look the fucking same.

Johnny Pete – where the fuck was this bus stop?

Frank Yeah, where the fuck was this fucking bus stop?

Pete How should I know?

Frank and Johnny laugh.

Top of Highgate Road.

Johnny Highgate Road!

Frank That means she's back at her dad's.

Johnny Has she finished college?

Frank She's finished college, she's back at her dad's, she's fresh like a peach, and it's all happening.

Johnny What time was this?

Pete How should I know?

Johnny Just tell me what fucking time it was!

Pete I'm sorry – I didn't keep a time-check.

Frank You'll never make a private dick.

Johnny Yeah – not like Philip Marlowe.

Pete What's got into you two . . .?

Johnny Was it morning? Afternoon? Evening? What?

Pete It was in the morning.

Johnny Like half past eight?

Pete Yeah, around that.

Frank Shit. That's early.

Johnny I don't care, I'm gonna be there.

Frank What dya mean?

Johnny The way I see it, she's got a job up west – Channel 4 most likely – and she gets the bus every day from the top of Highgate Hill. She's back in town, she's unattached – and I'm gonna party.

Frank Fuck it – I'm joining you.

Pete Yeah! Me too!

Frank So she's working at Channel 4?

Johnny Yeah. She's in charge of the peaches.

Pause.

Pete I saw her last week too as it goes.

Frank and Johnny look at Pete.

Johnny What!

Frank Where?

Pete Sainsbury's.

Johnny You saw Milly Foster at Sainsbury's? You kept that quiet!

Frank Yeah – you kept that fucking quiet.

Johnny Sainsbury's in Camden Town . . .? Pete . . .? Sainsbury's in Camden Town?

Pete Yeah.

Johnny Shit. Was she on her own?

Pete Yeah.

Frank and Johnny glance at each other.

Both *Wicked.*

Johnny Did she see you?

Pete Nah – I was in frozen foods, she was in baby care.

Johnny Baby care!

Frank You're joking!

Pete Nah.

Johnny You're joking?

Pete Yeah, I'm joking. She was in cereals.

Johnny Don't mess around . . . shit, I'm gonna start going to Sainsbury's. What day was this?

Pete I don't fucking know!

Johnny Well think about it – was it a weekend, a Monday, a Tuesday . . .?

Pete It was probably a Wednesday.

Frank Shit. I'm working on Wednesday.

Johnny What time?

Pete About three or four, maybe.

Johnny Three or four, Wednesday – you sure?

Frank Couldn't you make it a Thursday? I'm free all day Thursday.

Pete Alright then – it was a Thursday.

Frank What time?

Johnny What dya mean Thursday! I'm busy on Thursdays!

Frank Too bad.

Pete Come to think of it, I think it was Friday.

Frank Friday?

Johnny Well make up your mind!

Pete Or maybe it was Saturday? Did I say Sainsbury's? Sorry, I meant to say Waitrose, or maybe it was Asda? No

– it was definitely Tesco's. And it wasn't Milly, it was Billy
– Billy Bishop from Basingstoke. Or was it Willy? You
know – little Willy from Stamford Hilly.

*Pete walks over and hands Frank the shirt. Frank sits up
and puts it on.*

Johnny Pete – you shoulda pulled over.

Pete puts on his strides.

Pete I see quite a few old faces as it goes – I saw Julia in
Swiss Cottage.

Frank looks at Pete.

Frank She's fucking crazy for you.

Pete She ain't?

Frank Johnny – tell him.

Johnny looks at Pete.

Johnny She was asking Anna all about you – whether you
were still seeing Petra.

Pete You're kidding! How dya know?

Johnny Murray told me.

Pete How does he know?

Frank Ronnie told him.

Pete How the fuck does Ronnie know!?

Johnny His old man's ex-girlfriend's best mate's auntie's
neighbour's cousin met Suzie in a wine bar in Plumstead.

Pete How does Suzie know?

Johnny It's a long story.

Frank Yeah – it's a fucking long story.

Pete Shit. She's really cool . . . isn't she going out with Larry?

Frank They split up. Larry's going out with Kelly.

Pete I thought Kelly was with Alex?

Johnny Nah – Alex is checking Amy.

Pete Shit. I always liked Amy.

Frank Yeah – I was well gutted.

Pete sits down on the sofa beside Frank and puts on his shoes. Johnny walks over to the ironing board.

Johnny I saw Alice recently.

Frank and Pete look at Johnny.

Frank Where?

Johnny In Pimlico. She asked me round for dinner.

Frank Oh yeah?

Johnny Yeah, I couldn't believe my luck – I bought a new shirt and everything. I even shaved!

Pete Holy shit! So what happened?

Johnny She starts asking me all these weird questions.

Frank Like what?

Johnny Like if I ever had a gay experience.

Frank You're joking!

Johnny No.

Frank What did you say?

Johnny I told her about something that happened when I was nine.

Frank Oh yeah? What?

Johnny Nothing . . . it's not important.

Frank and Pete glance at each other.

Frank What did she say?

Johnny She told me she was gay.

Frank You're joking!

Pete Shit! So many women are gay these days. It makes me wanna cry.

Frank I know. Rachel had a scene with Lisa.

Johnny You're joking!

Frank For six months!

Johnny How dya know?

Frank Kate told me.

Johnny How does Kate know?

Frank She had a scene with Rachel.

Pete You're joking! Shit!

Frank So what happened with Alice?

Johnny It got really weird.

Frank How come?

Johnny Well, I was a tad peeved off to say the least – I mean I'd spent all my dole money on this new shirt and some Old Spice. I thought she was well outa line . . . anyway it turns out she's a real man-hater – she starts coming for me with the bread knife!

Frank You're joking! What's her fucking problem?

Johnny (*gestures innocently*) She thinks we've all got one track minds.

Frank and Pete stare incredulously.

Frank You're joking . . .!

Pete The fucking cheek!

Frank That the living lick or what?

Pete Fucking crazy bitch.

Frank You're joking!

Pete The fucking cheek!

Frank That the living lick or what?

Pete Fucking crazy bitch.

Johnny I know – crazy innit. (*He walks round behind the sofa and leans on it.*)

Frank So what happened?

Johnny Well after that we kinda run outa conversation . . . the food weren't all that either – turns out she's a vegan as well.

Pete Fuck that.

Johnny We had lentil soup followed by lentil stew followed by lentils for pudding. She asked me if I was sorry I came.

Frank What dya say?

Johnny I lied. If I'd told her the truth she'd have strangled me.

SCENE THREE

NW8. Crockers Folly pub. Vodka and orange, grapefruit and soda. Frank and **Pippa** *are sitting at a table.*

Pippa So, any gossip?

Frank Nothing – it's been a dry season.

Pippa You must have something.

Frank Not really . . . well . . . there was something . . .

Pippa What?

Frank No, it don't matter.

Pippa What is it?

Frank I can't tell you.

Pippa Why not? What is it?

Frank Well . . . you know that girl Cherry?

Pippa Yeah.

Frank Well . . . forget it, I shouldn't be telling you . . .

Pippa What is it? She's told you she's in love with you? She pines for you every day?

Frank No. Nothing like that.

Pippa Well what is it then?

Pause.

Frank Well, *yeah* basically.

Pippa I knew it.

Frank What dya mean, you knew it?

Pippa It was obvious.

Frank How?

Pippa The way she looked at you.

Frank What you talking about?

Pippa A woman just knows these things Frank.

Frank Yeah – I'm beginning to believe it.

Pippa So what happened?

Frank Well, we were at this nightclub in Leeds and . . . shit, I can't be saying this to you . . .

Pippa Why not?

Frank It ain't cool.

Pippa *You* ain't cool.

Frank Thanks.

Pippa So you were at this nightclub in Leeds . . .?

Frank Yeah. And she comes up to me and tells me.

Pippa Tells you what?

Frank Tells me she likes me. Since the First Year. How she had a breakdown about it.

Pippa She had a breakdown?

Frank Yeah. She OD'd on Valium – they had to pump her stomach out.

Pippa You're joking! B/cos of you!?

Frank Yeah. I have that effect on women. I can't help it.

Pippa Yeah yeah.

Frank Serious (*laughs*).

Pippa So? Do you like her?

Frank She's alright – I mean she's a friend, I don't think of her like that. Her aunt on the other hand . . .

Pippa Her aunt?

Frank Her aunt's a real peach.

Pippa Her aunt!

Frank Yeah. Her whole family in fact – except her dad of course.

Pippa Of course.

Frank And her grandad. I mean I don't want you to get the wrong idea.

Pippa So what did you say?

Frank What could I say? I didn't say nothing. The funny thing is, all the time I've know her all she's ever talked about is this guy Justin – it's been Justin this and Justin that and Justin don't kiss me in public and Justin don't hold my hand. He had a girlfriend you see, but she carried on with him for eighteen months – he treated her like shit but she was besotted by him. I heard so much about this Justin fella I almost felt like smacking him.

Pippa Why didn't you?

Frank He was six feet ten. Johnny says if a girl starts talking to you about that stuff you know she's interested.

Pippa Well Johnny's full of shit.

Frank That's what Pete says. He reckons it's the other way round.

Pippa Pete's full of shit as well.

Frank That's what I said. As far as I'm concerned all women are up for it – it's as simple as that. Some talk to you some don't – it don't make an ounce of difference.

Pippa You talk more shit than any of them.

Frank (*laughs*) Anyway, she's started sending me these letters.

Pippa Letters?

Frank Yeah, telling me what a great guy I am. I wrote back and said I already knew. I swear she thinks I'm God or something.

Pippa What does she say?

Frank She says she likes the way I do things – the way I walk . . . the way I talk . . . the way I smoke! I swear Pippa the girl's obsessed. She even wrote a story about me!

Pippa A story?

Frank Yeah . . . I'm this . . . little prince with magic powers . . . and I go to this . . . castle in the sky where the king's . . . having a banquet. Anyway something happens, I can't remember, and everyone freaks out, so I cast a spell on everything and . . . it all turns purple. The whole fucking castle! It all goes fucking purple! Before long the whole world's purple and everyone's happy. It's fucking crazy!

Pippa Aah, I think that's sweet.

Frank Sweet!? It's insane! I mean who ever heard of things turning purple!? Who ever heard of castles in the sky?

Pippa Jimi Hendrix.

Frank What?

Pippa Jimi Hendrix – he wrote a song called castles in the sky.

Frank Yeah but that's different.

Pippa What's different about it?

Frank He was a pop star for Christ's sake.

Pippa So?

Frank Besides, it's castles *made of sand* – don't you know nothing about nothing?

Pippa Castles in the sky, castles made of sand – it's the same thing.

Frank The same thing! How can you say that? It's a totally different thing completely! I mean castles made of sand *exist*, they're real, kids make them on the beach! Castles in the sky is *bullshit*, it's fantasy, it's . . . it's abstract!

Pippa So what? Picasso was abstract.

Frank Yeah but Picasso was Picasso! Cherry's Cherry – I mean Cherry ain't Picasso! Picasso was a fucking artist!

Pippa So? Maybe Cherry's an artist.

Frank Cherry ain't no artist Pippa, let me tell ya. She can't even spell properly – you should see where she puts her commas!

Pippa That don't mean anything.

Frank Shit. So now you're saying she's the new Picasso?

Pippa Don't be stupid, Picasso was a painter – maybe she's a writer.

Frank So you're saying she's the new Raymond Chandler?

Pippa Don't be stupid Frank – Chandler wrote crime, Cherry writes fairy tales.

Frank Too fucking right. Her whole life's a fairy tale – she thinks I'm gonna marry her!

Pippa You should be flattered.

Frank I am flattered. I just wish she'd go easy on the letters – they're doing my head in.

Pippa Aah, you poor thing . . . it's all related though Frank, can't you see that?

Frank What's related?

Pippa Well, these letters and this guy Justin.

Frank What you talking about?

Pippa She's like me – she wants what she can't have. She carried on with Justin even though he had someone else, the worse he treated her the more she wanted him.

Frank Don't be stupid!

Pippa It's true. Now she's fixed on you but she knows you've got Chrissie – that's the attraction. She only wants you b/cos she can't have you.

Frank She wants me b/cos I'm a groovy guy.

Pippa Frank, get real – you're about as groovy as a dead moth. If you were single she wouldn't wanna know.

Frank That's bullshit. You're just jealous cos no-one writes stories about you. I mean maybe she is an artist and she's gonna be super famous – kids all over the world will know about my magic powers. They'll set up a fan club. I'll have to have a bodyguard . . .

Pippa Don't talk piffle. Cherry's no artist, you said so yourself – she's just got a few problems that's all. I'm reading this book about it – women who love too much.

Frank You should read women who talk too much.

Pippa Frank, don't be upset.

Frank Upset! Me!? What the fuck makes you fucking think I'm fucking upset!?

Pippa Don't be like that Frank – I'm only trying to help you see things more clearly. A person should be aware of

themselves. Take me for instance, I'm the same as Cherry –
I'm always going for the wrong guys. Why else would I go
for you? No offence.

Frank Shit! You're even more in love with me than
Cherry. I shoulda realized.

Pippa Don't be silly Frank – you're the last person I'd fall
in love with. No offence. Women like me just want what's
forbidden, it's a recurring pattern, we don't learn from our
mistakes. It's all in this book.

Frank You and your books! Life ain't about books Pippa,
it's about the real world, it's about getting up in the
morning, it's about chicks and babes – it's about peaches!
Books are just a distraction . . .

Pippa Fine. Anyway, according to this book, we're seeking
love where we know we can't find it – apparently it's to do
with our fathers.

Frank That's right, blame your old man – I mean he only
worked his balls off to keep you in comfort. And that's the
thanks he gets.

Pippa It's good to confront the root of your problems
Frank, that way you learn about yourself – that's why I'm
in therapy.

Pause.

Frank You're in therapy?

Pippa Yeah. You should try it.

Frank Don't be daft, I got no call for it! I mean what
would a guy like me want with therapy? The way I see it,
the more you think about yourself the more fucked-up you
become. 'Keep your mind off your mind' – that's what
Joseph Cotten said.

Pippa laughs.

Johnny told me.

Pippa And what makes Joseph Cotten so clever?

Frank He was an actor!

Pippa So?

Frank Actors know their shit.

Pippa Since when?

Frank You can't be a big film star and not know your shit Pippa.

Pippa Says who?

Frank It's common knowledge.

Pippa Besides – most actors ain't film stars.

Frank Joseph Cotten was.

Pippa Most actors are out of work.

Frank That's b/cos they're all in therapy.

Pippa You talk crap.

Frank The truth hurts don't it.

Pippa Truth! What would you know about truth?

Frank I know that it's precious.

Pause.

Pippa You're the one that's precious.

SCENE FOUR

NW6. VW Polo. **Rob** *is driving, Frank is in the passenger seat.*

Rob Check it out.

Frank What?

Rob The blonde.

Frank What blonde? Where?

Rob There.

Frank Where?

Rob At the lights.

Frank I don't see no blonde.

Rob Over there!

Frank Where?

Rob You missed her. Too bad – she was living!

Frank What? You mean she was living?

Rob Yeah.

They laugh.

Fuck! Look at that!

Frank What?

Rob The brunette in that Saab.

Frank What Saab?

Rob The black Saab. Shit! Take a look at that!

Frank What?

Rob The redhead.

Frank Where?

Rob Coming out the flats.

Frank The black Saab?

Rob She's a piece of work.

Frank She ain't brunette. Are you sure it was a Saab?

Rob See that black chick!

Frank What redhead?

Rob Shit! Look at her mate! Look at that Chinese babe . . . shit!

Frank The redhead in the green dress?

Rob Holy fuck! Frank! Look at this!

Frank What? Where? Which black chick?

Rob Shit! That's it, I'm in love!

Frank Rob, look at the road will ya.

Rob Shit! Look at her body move! Frank!

Frank Rob! Look at the fucking road!

Rob turns to look at the road.

Rob Just checking out the sights Frankie . . . *shit! Clap your eyes on that!*

Frank What?

They look at each other and laugh. Pause.

Rob I saw Paul the other day.

Frank Paul?

Rob You know – Paul Simpson.

Frank Oh yeah.

Rob He took me to that massage parlour on West End Lane.

Frank Oh yeah? Go there a lot does he?

Rob I don't think so. It was mad.

Frank How come?

Rob It was fucking mad!

Frank How come?

Rob Well we go in, and this girl asks us if we want 'massage' . . .

Frank Yeah.

Rob We say no, just a sauna and jacuzzi. You shoulda seen her face, she was so pissed off – it was hilarious.

Frank Why was she pissed off?

Rob You don't go to those places for a sauna and jacuzzi Frank.

Frank You can if you want to.

Rob You can if you want to but they don't like it.

Frank Tough luck on them.

Rob I know. Anyway we walk through this lounge area to the sauna and there's all these girls in skimpy red skirts sitting around filing their nails.

Frank Oh yeah? What were they like?

Rob They were alright. This one girl says we can have who we like.

Frank You're joking!

Rob No.

Frank What did you say?

Rob We said we're not having 'massage'.

Frank What did she say?

Rob She was so pissed off. It was so funny.

Frank So they let you pick?

Rob Yeah.

Frank What were they like?

Rob They were alright.

Frank So what happened then?

Rob Well, as we're changing, this girl comes in and starts tarting herself up in the mirror.

Frank You're joking!

Rob No. She turns round and asks us if we want 'any extras'.

Frank Any extras?

Rob Yeah, you know – 'additional services'.

Frank Additional services?

Rob Yeah.

Frank Shit. What was she like?

Rob She was alright.

Frank What did you say?

Rob We said no.

Frank Shit. What was she like?

Rob She was alright.

Frank What did you say?

Rob We said no.

Frank What did she say?

Rob She just put her lipstick away and walked out.

Frank Was she pissed off?

Rob She was reeling.

  Pause.

Frank So what happened?

Rob Nothing. We had our sauna and jacuzzi and fucked off.

Frank How much?

Rob A tenner.

Frank That's not bad.

Rob That's cheap – it's the rest that's expensive.

Frank Like how much?

Rob I don't know!

  Pause.

Frank Shit.

Rob What's up?

Frank Nothing . . . just you . . .

Rob What?

Frank The things you get up to.

  Rob looks at Frank.

Rob When you ever gonna learn Frank?

Frank Learn what?

Rob Learn to enjoy yourself. How many times have I told
ya – life's too short, so you better get to work.

  Frank silently mimics Rob word for word.

There's no point being old, saying you lived a little, talking
about the fucking war! You gotta talk about *babes* when

Shop Assistant Can I help you?

Frank Yeah. I wanna buy a jacket.

Shop Assistant Do you know what kind?

Frank Yeah – those over there.

Shop Assistant Any particular colour?

Frank Green.

The shop assistant pulls a jacket off the rack and hands it to Frank.

Shop Assistant There you are, try that on.

Frank puts it on.

Frank Where's the mirror?

Shop Assistant Over there at the back.

They walk towards the mirror. Frank looks at himself.

How does it look?

Frank I don't know – it feels a bit big, have you got one a size down?

Shop Assistant That's the only one in green I'm afraid – we've got a smaller one in black.

Frank No. It's gotta be green.

The shop assistant laughs.

What dya reckon?

Shop Assistant I think it suits you – they're meant to hang down a bit you know, that's the style.

Frank Yeah . . . I'm not so sure.

Shop Assistant I'd say that's the right size, honestly – you've got to wear it more over your shoulders.

Frank pushes the jacket off his shoulders.

Frank Like that?

Shop Assistant Here, let me do it.

The shop assistant pulls the jacket over his shoulders and adjusts it.

That's better, see – that looks good!

Frank Yeah, that looks alright . . . I'm still not sure . . . it's not quite what I had in mind, it's a bit flimsy – have you got anything else similar?

Shop Assistant In green . . .? Not really.

Frank studies the jacket in the mirror.

Frank It's a bit too flimsy – don't ya think?

Shop Assistant What do you mean, flimsy?

Frank I mean a bit too baggy, you know . . . it don't hug around my body like it should.

They laugh.

Shop Assistant It's not that type of jacket. I think it looks good – it all depends what you want it for.

Frank What I want it for?

Shop Assistant Yeah, where you want to wear it – do you want to wear it just casual, in the street, or do you want it for going out?

Frank I just want a jacket.

Shop Assistant Well then, it's perfect! You can wear it anywhere! It looks good in the pub, and it looks good in the clubs. You're probably like me, I don't dress up to go out either – when I go to clubs I dress the same as I am now, pretty much. I'm hopeless!

Frank I wouldn't say that.

They laugh.

Dya go to clubs often?

Shop Assistant When I'm in the mood. What about you?

Frank Not really. I prefer to stay at home – put my feet up, put the kettle on and watch Songs of Praise.

The shop assistant laughs.

I've had my day out in the sun.

Shop Assistant You're not old!

Frank I feel old. Look at my grey hair. (*He bends down to show her his hair.*)

Shop Assistant What grey hair?

Frank There at the top.

Shop Assistant I think I can see *one*. Maybe two. That's nothing! You should see my brother!

Frank What about your sister?

Shop Assistant My sister? She's a bit young – she's only five!

Frank You're right, that is a bit young – even for Micky Bainbridge.

Shop Assistant I'm sorry?

Frank Don't apologize, it ain't your fault.

Shop Assistant You've lost me.

Frank I'm always losing things. Everything I ever had, I lost. Look – I'm even losing my hair! (*He pulls his hair back to reveal his hairline.*) You see – my hairline's receding.

Shop Assistant Don't be so silly, you're just paranoid! Besides, you're only as old as you feel.

Frank Is that right?

Shop Assistant Of course it is. How old are you? Twenty-four? Twenty-five?

They stare at each other.

Frank How much is this jacket?

They laugh.

Shop Assistant Doesn't it say?

Frank I don't think so.

Shop Assistant Hold on, I'll just ask the boss.

The shop assistant walks off. Frank studies himself in the mirror. The shop assistant walks on.

He says they're forty pounds normally but he'll let you have it for twenty-five.

Frank How come?

Shop Assistant B/cos it's the last one and we're almost closing.

Frank So they change price according to the time?

Shop Assistant Not really – he's just in a generous mood today.

Frank Why's that?

Shop Assistant I don't know, he just is – he's usually a grumpy sod. You should count yourself lucky – I bought one almost identical to that for seventy pounds last month.

Frank Seventy quid! Shit. Where was that?

Shop Assistant West End.

Frank Shit, that's a lot of money . . . mind you, anything's a lot of money to me at the moment.

Shop Assistant Things a bit tight are they?

Frank Just a bit.

Shop Assistant Well then, there you go.

Frank There you go what?

Shop Assistant There you go – you can't ignore a bargain like this. You've got to make the most of your opportunities.

Frank That's what I say. Life's too short, and there ain't enough time – so you better get to work.

Shop Assistant (*laughs*) So, what's the verdict?

    Pause.

Frank I can't make up my mind. I'm so indecisive these days it's a joke . . .

Shop Assistant Why's that?

Frank I don't know. Usually I don't mess around . . .

Shop Assistant Maybe you're under stress.

Frank Stress. That's it. It's hitting me from every angle.

Shop Assistant You need to relax a bit – go out for a nice drink with someone.

Frank I tried it, every night for the past month – it don't help. What I really need is a massage. How you fixed?

Shop Assistant Why, you cheeky . . .!

Frank (*laughs*) Just being friendly.

Shop Assistant So – what about the jacket?

Frank What jacket?

The shop assistant laughs.

I'm still not sure . . .

Shop Assistant It looks good on you, it really does.

Frank Dya think so?

Shop Assistant Yeah. I do.

Frank Thanks.

Shop Assistant Don't mention it.

They laugh.

It's good quality as well – it's made of viscose.

Frank Viscose? What's that?

Shop Assistant I don't really know to be honest.

They laugh.

It's a bit like silk.

Frank Right.

They laugh.

It still feels too big.

Shop Assistant They're meant to be big. Here, let me show you – give me the jacket.

Frank takes off the jacket and hands it to the shop assistant. She puts it on and poses in the mirror.

Frank That looks good.

Shop Assistant You see. If I didn't already have one I'd probably buy this.

Frank You can have it for thirty quid.

The shop assistant laughs.

Where you from? Birmingham?

Shop Assistant Yeah! How did you guess?

Frank Whereabouts in Birmingham?

Shop Assistant Well, Wolverhampton really.

Frank Shit. How come?

Shop Assistant I was born there!

They laugh.

Frank What brings you down here?

Shop Assistant I just wanted to spend the summer here, while I'm waiting for my exam results.

Frank What exams?

Shop Assistant My A Levels.

Frank Your A Levels! How old are you?

Shop Assistant Seventeen.

Frank Seventeen! You're joking!

Shop Assistant No.

Frank Shit. Seventeen . . . you're joking!

Shop Assistant No.

Frank Shit. And what you gonna do after?

Shop Assistant Go to college.

Frank Where?

Shop Assistant Hopefully London – it depends on my grades.

Frank What subject?

Shop Assistant Child psychology.

Frank Shit.

The shop assistant takes off the jacket.

So where you staying?

Shop Assistant Hackney.

Frank Hackney!

Shop Assistant Yeah – do you know it?

Frank Everyone I know lives in Hackney.

Shop Assistant Really?

Frank Yeah. You staying at a mate's?

Shop Assistant That's right.

Frank I see.

Shop Assistant You see what?

Frank Nothing – I just see, that's all.

They laugh. The shop assistant offers Frank the jacket.

Shop Assistant So – have you made up your mind?

Frank Yeah.

Shop Assistant And . . .?

Frank I don't want it.

Shop Assistant Why not?

Frank It's too big. I reckon you should buy it.

Shop Assistant How can it be too big for you if it's okay for me?

Frank That's different.

Shop Assistant Why's it different?

Frank You know . . .

Shop Assistant No.

Frank You're a woman.

Shop Assistant So?

Frank I'm a man.

Shop Assistant And?

Frank It's different, that's all. Women can wear things big, it looks cool, blokes it looks like they bought the wrong size. We're different shapes, I mean you musta noticed. Our minds are different, we talk about different things – girls talk about castles in the sky, guys talk about sand castles – things that *exist*! Girls talk about books, guys talk about peaches . . .!

Shop Assistant Peaches?

Frank That's it! That's all they talk about! Peaches – pure and simple. Okay, they might talk about other things, but they're thinking about . . .

Shop Assistant Peaches.

Frank You got it.

Shop Assistant So that's all you think about is it?

Frank Not me personally – I'm just talking in general . . .

  They laugh.

Shop Assistant So what about you – what do you think about?

Frank I don't know – lots of stuff.

Shop Assistant Like what?

Frank What?

Shop Assistant What do you think about?

Frank Millions of things.

Shop Assistant Say one.

Pause.

Frank What, other than peaches?

The shop assistant nods her head. Pause.

I can't think straight – could we discuss it over a drink?

Afterword

so the phone rang – it was tuesday – it was
james – the director – he said 'nick i wanna
say something'
i said 'james say what you like mate i won't
say nothing'
he said 'fine' – but it was the way he said it
– 'fine' – just like that
2 months later the phone rang again
'hello' said a voice
'hello' said mine
'it's robin, you know, robin hooper – my
friends call me gary cooper or minnie the
moocha'
it was a riveting conversation
he said 'write 300 words for the programme i'll
give ya 30 quid'
i got out my pocket calculator – that's 6 quid
a word i thought i'll do it – then i realized i'd
pressed the wrong button – i've been had i
thought – had like a kipper – never trust a
bloke called minnie
so i rang stephen daldry – the artistic doodah
– i said 'stephen'
he said 'just call me stephen, darling'
i said 'just call me darling, stephen'
he said 'just call me frederico'
i said 'freddie there seems to be a problem'
'what's that freddie?' he asked
i said 'i was hoping you would tell me'
so he told me

so i rang lisa makin – the casting director –
i said 'lisa i've been cast'
she said 'you won't be the last'
'they want a spiel'
'it's a good deal – 10p a word – that's class'
'but i'm worth more than . . . surely . . . you
can't put a price on . . .'
'alright' she said, 'i'll do it'
fuck off
i rang david roger – the dodger – i said – 'oi
dave do us a fave'
he said no
i said 'don't be ashamed'
he said no
i said 'say yes or no'
he said no
so i hit him
it was wednesday – the phone rang – i jumped
outa bed – bumped my head – it was the
president of venezuela – he wanted a cab – i
said i'd be there in 10 minutes
he wanted to go to putney – he'd heard about it

Nick Grosso
May 1995

THE KNOCKY

Michael Wynne

Characters

Rory, Gary's friend
Gary Malone, Mary's 11-year-old son
Steven Kelly, 12-year-old son
Mrs MacNally, a neighbour
Norma Kelly, mother
Joseph Kelly, 20-year-old son
Pete Malone, Joseph's friend
Lizzie Kelly, 18-year-old daughter
Tommy Kelly, father
Gwen Malone, Norma's middle sister
Mary Malone, Norma's younger sister
Detective Inspector Tower, a policeman
Police Constable Buck, a policeman
Pearl Malone, Norma, Mary and Gwen's mother

The Knocky was first performed at the Royal Court Theatre Upstairs on 13 October 1994 with the following cast:

Pearl/Mrs MacNally Annie Hayes
Pete/PC Buck Jonathan McGuinness
Steven James Beattie
Joseph Andy Snowden
Mary/Gary Elizabeth Berrington
Norma Eileen O'Brien
Tommy/Rory/DI Tower Derek Howard
Lizzie Sarah-Jane Potts
Gwen was played by various members of the cast

Director Jane Collins
Designer Halinka Fraser
Lighting Kevin Sleep

The Knocky was revived at the Royal Court Theatre Upstairs on 16 February 1995, and then on tour. The cast included: Helen Blatch (**Pearl/Mrs MacNally**), Adrian Bower (**Pete/PC Buck**), Stuart Callaghan (**Steven**), Richard Henders (**Joseph**), Felicity Montagu (**Mary/Gary**), Eileen O'Brien (**Norma**), Michael O'Connor (**Tommy/Rory/DI Tower**) and Lynda Thornhill (**Lizzie**). *Director*: Brian Stirner. *Designer*: Robin Don. *Lighting*: Kenneth Parry.

The action takes place on an estate in Birkenhead, in the summer of 1994.

Act One

SCENE ONE

Complete darkness. Small tent in the middle of the stage, the side facing the audience. Any other scenery is not visible. The only light is from a strong torch inside the tent, which flickers, the characters silhouetted against the canvas. We can see the shapes of three people sitting round inside the tent. The tent should seem as if it is in the countryside.

Three young boys' voices are heard. **Gary, Rory** *and* **Steven.** *Gary has the torch.*

Rory Will you shine the torch over here, I'm gonna spill me soup.

Gary All right. All right, it keeps flickering, though.

The light goes off.

Rory Aah shit. I've poured it all in me sleeping bag now. You did that on purpose.

Gary No I didn't, the Sellotape keeps coming loose.

The light comes back on.

Rory Aah, look at that, cream of chicken soup all over me undies. What's me mum gonna think I've been up to?

Gary I dunno. What do y' want to bring a big flask of chicken soup with y' for anyway?

Rory That's what you do when you go camping, don't y'. A sleeping bag, marshmallows round the camp fire and a flask of something hot. Eh, and this flask is a special one. Me mum told me, it keeps hot stuff cold and, er, cold stuff hot.

Gary I've got Chewitts – are they like marshmallows?

Steven (*had enough of them and taking control again*) Will youse two stop farting about and let me finish this story?

Rory Yeah, go on, go on, we're listening.

Steven So she's all alone in the car in the middle of the woods, when there's this big banging on the roof. (*He bangs the flask three times slowly.*) Like someone's head buttin' it.

Gary What was it?

Steven I'm gonna tell y' now. So she's sitting there bricking herself when all these police cars with sirens and flashing lights turn up. They make a big line across the road, and the bloke in charge has one of those loud hailer things and says, dead posh like: 'Slowly get out of the car and whatever you do don't turn round.' She gets out and he keeps saying, 'Don't look round,' and she walks towards the police. Oh, and that banging on the car is still banging. (*bangs three times*) She gets in front of the police and guess what?

Gary They shoot her.

Steven Shut up, will y'. No, she turns round doesn't she and she sees . . . (*The torch goes off.*) You did that on purpose.

Gary No, I didn't. What does she see?

Steven She sees . . . Oh, who's that?

Rory It was me.

Steven That stinks. Can you try and keep it in your sleeping bag? It's not that scary. (*The torch comes back on.*) It's wafting over 'ere, look, green smoke.

We see the silhouette of Steven wafting his arm about.

Rory No, it's not, what does she see?

Gary Who?

Steven (*ignoring him, tuts*) She turns round and there's this nutter standing on top of the car with her boyfriend's head in his hands, whacking it on the roof.

Rory Nooo. Is that true?

Steven Yeah, it happened just up the road, y'know, by Tam o' Shanter's Cottage.

Rory Gaad.

Gary Was he dead?

Steven What d'you think? Aah, you've done it again. That's the eggiest boff I've ever smelt.

Rory I can't help it.

Gary What did he do with the rest of him, y'know, his body?

Steven It doesn't matter. Right, shall we go outside in a minute?

Rory Naah, I don't feel like it tonight.

Steven You're scared, aren't y'?

Rory No, I'm not, I just, just don't want to.

Steven Are you coming out, Gary?

Gary D'yer reckon he used a knife or just ripped it off with his bare hands?

Steven What?

Gary That bloke's head.

Steven I'm gonna rip your head off in a minute.

Steven grabs Gary's head and takes the torch off him.

Come on, let's go up to Biddie Hill. As long as we don't split up, we won't get our heads battered. And look we'll be able to see, 'cause the torch is working all right now. (*It goes off.*) Great. Aah, come on, we don't need this, anyway. (*He unzips the tent and throws the torch out.*) We can go out and do the Grand National across all the hedges.

Rory Er . . . it's better doing it during the day 'cause then we might, might get chased by someone. And will you close that flap, I don't want the hairy *hand* monster coming in.

Steven Don't be soft. (*He zips it up.*)

Rory It's all right for you, you're in the middle.

Gary I know, I like it here.

Rory Not you, divvy, you're not in the middle, you're on the outside like me.

Gary Oh, so I am.

Steven So what if I'm in the middle?

Rory Well, I've got more chance of finding a hairy hand in me sleeping bag or being stabbed or something.

Steven Well, if we go out for a bit, you can go in the middle when we get back.

Rory Er . . . OK. We'll go in a minute.

Pause.

Gary Why don't we piss through someone's letter box?

Steven Naah, that's tight.

Gary Your Joseph used to do it.

Steven (*very defensive*) My brother wouldn't do that.

Silence. Pause. Then, a dog howls.

Rory Did you hear that?

Gary What?

Rory It sounded like a howl.

Steven It's probably only a wolf.

Rory You don't get wolves round here.

Gary I saw one the other week.

Rory Did yer?

Gary Yeah, you were with me.

Rory That wasn't a wolf, it was a poodle.

Gary No, it wasn't, it was a white wolf.

Rory Since when do wolves have red ribbons in their hair?

Gary That was blood.

Rory Why would some little old lady keep a pet wolf?

Gary I've told you, haven't I. She's a witch. I've seen her burying things in the garden and she had this big book of spells with her.

Steven So anyone who has a poodle and does a bit of gardening is a witch, then?

Gary (*confused*) Yeah?

We hear a throaty cough.

Rory Did you hear that?

All listen.

Gary What?

Another cough, accompanied by loud footsteps.

Rory Now that was definitely someone and they're coming this way. I hope it's not that nutter looking for a new head to play with.

Gary Maybe that witch has heard us and she's coming to turn us into chip butties and then she'll feed us to her wolf and . . .

Steven Shush. Whatever it is, it's coming through the gate.

A yellow street lamp flickers into action, it lights up the whole stage. We can now see the tent is not in the countryside but in a small garden, the grass no wider than the tent. A path on the right leads to the back door of a council house. There is a window on the left, two bedroom windows and a small bathroom window above with high fences both sides. Entering the garden is **Mrs MacNally.** *She is middle-aged, very drunk and in the wrong garden.*

Rory Quick, get the torch.

Steven You.

Rory No, you.

Gary I'll get it.

Rory Quick.

Gary puts his hand out and pulls the torch back in.

Steven Why did you want the torch?

Rory Er . . . I dunno.

Steven Don't put it on or it'll know we're awake.

Rory It doesn't work, anyway.

Steven Whatever it is, it's in the garden.

Rory Let me in the middle.

Gary No, me.

Steven You're on me head. Don't you dare fart.

Mrs MacNally coughs and notices the tent.

Shush.

Mrs MacNally Eh. What the fuck's goin' on 'ere, eh?

Gary It's the witch.

Mrs MacNally Eh, youse lot can piss right off. I go the pub for a couple of bevvies and while I'm gone me garden's full of fuckin' squatters. Well, eh, you can all get out right now. Now. (*She attempts to open the tent but trips over a guy rope.*) You tricky little bastards, me garden's booby trapped.

Rory Quick, grab the zip so she can't get in.

They do, so does she. Gary switches the torch on and lights up the tent.

Steven No!

Rory Switch it off.

Gary It's stuck.

The torch flashes round inside the tent, we see them scrambling about trying to hide. They try to cover the torch with a sleeping bag but light leaks out.

Mrs MacNally I can see youse. I bet there's hundreds of yer in there, isn't there? I know my rights, y' fuckin' New Age travellers, what do y' think this is, Stonehenge? I'm not having a load of fuckin' soap-dodgers breeding in my garden.

Steven It's not the witch, it's Mrs MacNally from down the road. She's gone mad.

The upstairs bedroom light comes on. Mrs MacNally notices.

Mrs MacNally Eh, what's goin' on 'ere, eh? They're in me bloody bastard house now. Eh, get you and your joss sticks out of my house now.

The kitchen light comes on.

I've just had the place fuckin' decorated.

Norma *comes out in her dressing gown and slippers.*

Norma What's going on?

Mrs MacNally The fuckin' cheek of it. Have you settled in all right? Is it to your approval? D'yer like the wallpaper, George Henry Lees that is. (*She recognizes Norma.*) Oh, so it's you, eh, Norma Kelly? Not happy with having one house down the road, you move into my fuckin' house, too. Couldn't you fit them all in the house, eh? You've got some of them in me bloody garden as well.

Norma (*as if talking to a child*) Mrs MacNally. This is our house, you're in the wrong bloody garden. This is number fourteen, you live at number twenty.

Mrs MacNally Yeah?

Norma Yeah. (*showing her to the gate*) This way. Did they have a stay-behind at The Swan, did they?

Mrs MacNally Eh.

Norma There you go, d'yer think you'll find it this time?

Mrs MacNally Eh, yeah. Thanks, love.

She goes off right through the gate, Norma goes over to the tent.

Norma Are you kids all right? It was only Mrs MacNally from number twenty, pilatic as usual.

Rory Yeah.

Steven We're OK.

Norma I'll see youse in the morning. Goodnight.

Gary Goodnight.

Rory See yer.

Norma Has someone been farting?

Rory Er.

Steven Goodnight, mum.

She closes the zip, looks round the garden and goes back inside, locking the door. The kitchen light goes off.

I'm going to sleep now.

Rory What time is it?

Steven Ee are, pass us the torch. It's ten past one.

Gary Aren't we going out?

Steven I'm not now.

Rory Neither am I.

Steven We could later.

Gary Right then.

He bangs the torch, it goes off. The bedroom light also goes off. The lights change significantly to represent time passing.

SCENE TWO

A few hours later. Silence.

Steven Are youse asleep?

No answer.

Does that mean yeah? I'm dying for a wee.

> *He unzips the flap and puts his head out, looking left and right. He gets out of the tent and looks around the garden. He is just wearing shorts and T-shirt. He goes to the left-hand side of the tent. He wees in a plastic ornamental urn in the corner of the garden against the fence.*
>
> *Under the street lamp* **Joseph** *and* **Pete** *appear. Pete is smoking and Joseph wears very distinctive clothing (so that the audience will instantly recognize him when they see him again). Joseph is visibly quite nervous, Pete is pretty cool; this is certainly not the first time he has done this.*
>
> *Steven hears them talking and listens, he is not sure what is going on. He cannot quite hear what is being said.*

Joseph Listen, you just wait out here and I'll bring the stuff out to y'.

Pete OK. Go on, then.

Joseph You keep dixies, and watch upstairs in case they hear me.

> *Joseph stalls for a second, Pete is getting impatient.*

Pete Listen, mate, I'll do it.

Joseph We agreed I'd do it. So just . . . I know what to get and I know where I'll find it. So wait here.

Pete I'm waiting.

Steven is just about to go back into the tent when the gate opens. He hides on the left side of the tent. Joseph shines the torch around the garden. He goes over to the tent, as if about to open the flap, but he just listens. Steven realizes it is his brother and moves to get up and say something when Pete comes through the gate, so he hides back where he was. Joseph, seeing that Pete has come in, speeds up. He goes to the window, jars it open, breaking the frame as he does so, and climbs in. We see the torch flashing around inside the house, in the kitchen at one point. Steven looks towards the house and Pete not sure whether to move, but clearly horrified.

Joseph climbs out of the window with the video in his hands. He reaches back inside and pulls out more stuff. He puts the medal in his jeans pocket (where it stays for most of the play), family allowance book in another and he has a load of chicken legs wrapped in a tea towel. He walks through the garden and drops a chicken leg on the path.

Joseph 'Ere we are. (*He hands over the video and family allowance book.*) That's all they had.

Pete I said I wanted cash.

Joseph That's just as good, the book's nearly full. Come on, we're quits now.

Pete Are you sure there was no money?

Pete thinks briefly and then looks towards the house, giving Joseph the impression that he is going to go in himself. Joseph panics and gets out the medal.

Joseph They had this as well. I think it's valuable.

Pete (*Taking it off him and looking at it*) This shitty piece of medal. I wouldn't get anything for that, it's worthless. (*He throws it on to the grass.*) This'll have to do (*meaning the book*).

Joseph (*holding up the knotted tea towel bag of chicken legs*) D'yer want a chicken leg?

Pete (*as he leaves*) Don't give up your day job.

Joseph What day job?

Joseph pauses for a second and looks round the garden. He bends down and picks up the medal, looks at it and considers putting it back in the house. Steven slowly starts to stand up to say something. Joseph decides not to put it back and rushes out the gate, dropping another chicken leg by the gate on the way out. Steven doesn't have a chance to say anything. He goes to the gate to see if they've gone. He checks the broken window. He stands motionless in front of the tent for a moment, trying to make sense of what he has seen. As he's getting into the tent he hears someone coming, thinks they've come back and rushes in.

Lizzie runs in, wiping tears from her face. She leans on the fence for a minute trying to compose herself but breaks down again. She sniffs her clothes and retches, about to throw up. She runs into the house through the back door. We see the bathroom light go on almost immediately and can hear a shower running.

Steven looks out of the flap again towards the bathroom window and then lies down with the top half of him sticking out of the tent. He watches the stars in the sky and eventually falls asleep.

SCENE THREE

Early morning. The sun comes up. It is a really hot day

*with the sun beating down. Norma is up and about inside
the house. We can't see her.*

Norma (*shouting from inside*) Noooooo! (*She runs into
the kitchen and we can see her through the glass in the
back door. She struggles with the locks.*) They can get in,
but I bloody well can't get out. (*She opens the door and
runs out into the garden in a panic. She is wearing a
dressing gown and slippers. She runs over to the tent. She
sees Steven and thinks he's been hurt. She attempts to give
him mouth-to-mouth resuscitation to wake him up.*)
Steven . . . the sods . . . come on, son, wake up, wake up.

Steven (*waking up*) What's happening?

Norma Oh son, are you hurt? What did they do to you?

Steven (*confused*) I must have fallen asleep watching the
stars in the sky.

Norma Oh love, I thought you'd been hurt. We've been
broken into.

Steven I . . . er . . . have we?

Norma Did you see anything?

Steven (*slight pause*) No, no, nothing, nothing at all.

Norma I'm surprised they didn't see your head poking
out.

Steven Mmm . . . yeah.

Norma Are the others awake? Are you with us, Gary,
Rory?

Rory Hiya, Mrs Kelly.

Norma Gary?

Gary All right, Auntie Norma.

Norma You boys didn't see anything strange last night, did yer?

Gary Yeah, there was this drunk woman and she was . . .

Norma Yes, I know. I was here, then, Gary love.

Rory Nothing.

Norma Never mind, d'you boys want to come inside and have some breakfast?

Rory and **Gary** Yeah.

Norma Go on, then. Take your sleeping bags inside as well and put the telly on. Our Gwen's up, she'll give you some cereal. There's cornies or krispies. And don't touch anything 'cause we need fingerprints.

Rory Right.

They hop into the house with their sleeping bags right up to their shoulders. Gary has his on upside down with only his feet poking out. Rory has a large chicken soup stain on his sleeping bag.

Norma (*to Rory about the soup stain*) What's happened to your sleeping bag, love?

Rory I had a little accident.

Norma I can see that. (*shouting to Gary, as he's inside now*) Your mum should be coming over here in a minute, Gary, I'm just going to ring her. Eh, and no sliding down the stairs in them sleeping bags pretending to be caterpillars. (*to herself*) Our Gwen thought the triffids had come for her last time.

Steven gets up out of the tent. Norma walks over to look at the window but stands on the chicken leg.

The little . . . even me chicken legs for today's party. (*She picks it up and throws it over the fence on the right.*) Ooh, if I could get me hands on them.

Steven You all right, Mum?

Norma Yeah, come here, son. (*She holds him in front of her and ruffles his hair, trying to hide how upset she is.*) As long as you're all right, that's all the matters. (*pause*) You're sure you didn't see or hear anything strange last night?

Steven No. After Mrs MacNally had gone we all went straight to sleep.

Norma Oh well, I just thought you might have been able to help the police to find them.

Steven You're gonna phone the police?

Norma Of course.

Steven Will they catch them?

Norma You never know. There might be some good fingerprints inside.

  Short pause.

Steven What would happen to them, y'know, if they're caught? Would they go to prison?

Norma I don't know, son, let's hope so. A good stretch inside might sort them out.

Steven I . . . er . . .

Norma Well, at least the sun's out, they can't take that away from us, eh?

Steven Are we still gonna have the party for me nan?

Norma Yeah, yes, too right and it'll be the best garden party this street has ever seen. I'd better get me skates on. Will you take the tent down for me?

Steven Yeah.

Norma D'you want the other two to give you a hand?

Steven Naah, I'll do it meself.

Norma Right, what first, I'd better phone Mary and the police. (*She goes in.*)

Steven clears the last sleeping bag out of the tent, throws the torch on to the grass. It comes on. He takes out all the pegs and climbs inside. We can just make out someone saying something.

Tommy (*from inside the house, talking to* Norma) What d'you want?

Tommy Kelly *comes to the door and waits there. Norma appears behind him with the phone receiver on her shoulder mid phoning someone. She takes a pound from her purse and gives it to him.*

Norma A medium white sliced, pint of milk and a large onion. OK? (*She puts the receiver to her ear and goes back inside.*)

Tommy Yeah. (*under his breath but without any bitterness*) Keep the change.

He walks over and looks at the broken window. The poles inside the tent fall on Steven's head. Tommy (his dad) goes to help him but stands against the fence for a minute, watching. He goes to leave through the gate but Steven pops his head out, sees him and shouts to him. Tommy is redundant, in every sense of the word. Tommy finds it difficult to make conversation with his son and their brief chat should be a complete contrast to the previous dialogue between Steven and Norma.

Steven Dad! Where y' going?

*He gets out of the tent and continues to take it down.
Tommy does not help.*

Tommy The shop for y' mum. (*Pause. He waits for
another question.*) Were you warm enough in there?

Steven (*carrying on with the tent*) Yeah, it was boiling.

Tommy It's been a good tent, that. (*beat*) So you didn't see
anything then?

Steven Nothing.

Tommy Your mum'll be on to the police by now. I don't
see the point meself.

Steven What would happen to them if they were caught?

Tommy Dunno, son, probably send them to the Bahamas.

Steven I'd like to go there.

Tommy Wouldn't we all. I'd better be off.

Steven Are you coming back for me nan's party?

Tommy (*holding up the pound coin*) Yeah, or we won't
have enough butties. (*He goes.*)

*Steven finishes rolling up the tent and goes to walk
indoors. He stops, looks at the broken window and
decides to stay in the garden. He puts the rolled-up tent
at the bottom of the garden and lies across it looking at
the grass close up and seeing if there's any life.*

*There is a slight lighting change as the sun gets hotter
and brighter. This is to represent some more time
passing, as it is now later in the morning.*

*A figure appears in the downstairs front room
window through the net curtains. It is* **Gwen**; *she is
looking out into the garden.*

*Norma, wearing a skirt, blouse, apron and, as always,
a tea towel in her hand, comes out with a basket of
washing and starts to hang it on the line, on the right of
the path. The kitchen door remains open through the
rest of the play. We can just see a sink on the right-hand
side and a work surface opposite it where Norma
prepares food. There is a small step down to the path.*

Norma (*wiping along the line with a cloth*) This should
dry in no time. (*Steven not listening. She hangs up a pair
of boxer shorts. Norma talks to Gwen.*) See, I told you it
was a nice day, Gwen. Look, not a cloud in the sky. (*to
Steven*) Have you had any breakfast?

Steven (*in his own world*) Oh, no, I'll get some now.

Norma Gary and Rory are watching the telly in there.

Steven Yeah. (*He goes in.*)

*Norma continues to hang out the washing. Gwen moves
about in her window.* **Mary** *enters with a big bag and a
karaoke tape machine. She is wearing a summer dress
and scraping her sandal on the ground.*

Mary That is the last time I wear open-toed sandals round
'ere. Hiya, Nor. I've got dog shite all between me toes.

Norma Mary.

*Norma walks over to Mary, about to hug her. She
wants to talk about what has happened, but Mary is too
involved with her shoe.*

Oh Mary, they . . .

Mary Have you got a bucket of water or something, the
smell of this is making me wanna throw.

*Norma turns right round, picks up a bucket from
outside the back door and heads inside.*

Norma Yeah, OK.

Mary (*taking her sandal off and now prepared to talk about it*) So they took that video you'd just bought.

Norma (*from inside, filling up a bucket with water*) We'd only had it two days, it didn't even have a plug on it.

Mary The little scrots. Eh, I'll tell yer, you're lucky they didn't take anything else. I know people who've had the whole house stripped out, carpet and curtains as well.

Norma (*coming outside with the bucket*) They would've had a hard time finding anything else of any value. (*handing her the bucket*) Ee are.

Mary (*as she cleans her foot*) Were y' insured?

Norma What d'you think?

Mary Eh, I'll tell yer what. Some bloke came in the pub the other night with a video, dirt cheap it was. Even had a remote.

Norma I don't wanna know.

Mary Naah, he's all right, it's all above board. You can even order stuff off him.

Norma I don't care how cheap it was, I don't want anything dodgy in my house.

Mary Suit yerself. So we're still going ahead with the party?

Norma Of course we are, they're not gonna spoil me mother's day. I feel as if we've got more reason to have a good time, to show them that they can't defeat us. And I've got a kwish defrosting in there.

Mary A quiche.

Norma Yeah, yeah, whatever. Well, nothing else has

changed. We're still gonna surprise me mother and give her her war medal. So everything's going to plan.

Mary (*finishing cleaning her foot*) Aah, it is gonna be good, isn't it?

Norma I just can't get out of me head the thought that some little toe rag has been wandering round my house, uninvited. It's that just as much as the video going. D'yer know what I mean?

Mary (*pouring the dirty water into the ornamental urn while Norma watches, stunned*) It'll do these weeds some good, I'm sure dog crap has got just as much goodness in it as horse manure – think of all that marrowbone. I'll tell yer, I don't want to shit you up, girl, but it sounds like they knew what they were coming for. (*She goes inside, taking the bucket in and washing her hands in the sink.*)

Norma Tell me about it. They've probably got shares in Dixons and they get new addresses sent to them every time someone buys something. I wouldn't be surprised if they watched us carry it back from the shop. They should lock them up and not just throw away the key, but change the locks, just in case.

Mary (*coming back outside and drying her hands on the boxer shorts furthest away from Norma, so she doesn't see*) You know what I think. Until they bring back torture we're not safe in our beds.

Norma That's a bit extreme.

Mary No, I'm telling yer. They should get the stocks down in Birkenhead Market for petty stuff and if it keeps on happening, wheel out the rack and the thumbscrews.

Norma Oh, I dunno. What I'd say to them if I saw them . . . (*She goes to hang up some more washing and sees* *the other chicken leg by the gate. She picks it up, throws it over the fence and shouts.*) Bastards.

Mary Eh, that's it. Come on, be assertive, I saw it on *Oprah*. What you've got to do is scream your anger out.

Norma Yer wha'?

Mary Y'know, 'Swearing can be suitable.'

Norma Y'know I don't like swearing, Mary. I just think there's no need.

Mary Just try it. Come on, It'll free all your emotions. Right, repeat after me. (*She shouts.*) Bastards.

Norma (*not convinced, she continues to sort out the washing*) Bastards.

Mary Buggers.

Norma (*poking her head out from between the washing*) Buggers.

Mary (*gradually getting louder*) Sods.

Norma Sods.

Mary Shits.

Norma Shits.

Mary Arse holes.

Norma Arse holes.

  Dog on the right next door starts barking.

Mary (*getting carried away and screaming*) Wankers, twats, fuckers, dickheads, cunts . . .

Norma All right, all right. I think that's enough. You'll give Desmond next door a hernia. (*Dog still barking.*

Pause.) And you can fuck off as well. Quiet, Pavlov!
Pavlov!

It stops.

Mary Don't you feel better, though?

Norma They even took me chicken legs I'd cooked for
today.

Mary (*trying to be serious*) Chicken legs?

Norma Chicken legs.

They both burst out laughing.

Mary I hope they've got salmonella. (*She gets her
cigarettes out of her bag and notices the rolled-up tent on
the grass.*) Oh, my God, I forgot our Gary was stayed
here. I thought it was a bit quiet last night. (*She runs over
to the kitchen and shouts inside.*) You all right in there,
Gary lad? (*not waiting for a reply*) Good. (*She lights a
fag.*)

Norma hangs the rest of the washing out.

Nor, what have you told our Gwen? Does she know?

Norma No, and I'm not going to tell her either, it'd kill
her.

Mary But what about the window? (*which is still ajar*)
What does she think has happened to it?

Norma I told her your Gary was messing about last night
and he broke it.

Mary Oh, cheers. What are you going to say when the
police turn up?

Norma I'll say they've come to see . . . er . . . Gary.

Mary Cheers, Nor, he's only eleven and you've got him

down as Public Enemy Number One already. Shall we
print the Wanted posters now to save time?

Norma All right, I had to say something and she wouldn't
believe me if I said any of my kids had been involved with
the police.

Mary They're all so bloody perfect, aren't they?

Norma Oh, give me a break, will yer, you don't know
what it's like here, I have to go round whispering in case
she overhears anything that'll upset her. And now Lizzie's
taking lessons off her. And Tommy . . .

Mary Lizzie? What's wrong with her?

Norma I'll tell you in a minute, let me just go and put me
scones on. We'd better get ready for this party. (*She rushes
inside and starts preparing food.*)

Mary I suppose I'd better say hello. (*She goes over to
Gwen's window.*) Gwen, hiya girl, it's me, Mary, your
sister, you all right in there? Great. Bloody hell.

Tommy comes back with a bag of shopping.

Hiya, Thomas. Been shoplifting again?

Tommy Yeah, something like that.

*He goes into the kitchen and hands Norma the bag. She
looks inside.*

Norma (*from inside*) What sort of an onion is that?

Mary Eh, Nor, if you want anything doing, I'm here, just
give me a shout.

Norma Well . . .

Mary (*already decided that she's going to sunbathe, she
takes out a blanket or a rusty old sun lounger from the
corner of the garden and places it in the middle of the*

grass) I'm just gonna get a few of these rays first. This sun's bloody gorgeous. (*She takes off her dress, she is wearing a bikini underneath.*)

All through the next scene Norma is busy in the kitchen, talking to Mary from there, occasionally coming out. Mary sunbathes while talking and carries out a little ritual of smoking a fag, eating a bag of crisps, picking the crisps out of her teeth and then applying her suntan lotion.

Oh, I've brought the karaoke machine. Don't worry, I haven't got any Dionne Warwick, so me mother won't be singing.

Norma (*shouting out from inside the kitchen*) I don't want another re-run of Christmas. I couldn't get the bloody microphone off her.

Mary I tell yer, if I hear 'Walk On By' ever again, well, I just won't be responsible for me actions.

Norma And I don't want any of your fellas fighting either.

Mary It's all under control. Declan couldn't get bail, Richard's been deported and Jacques is back on the tablets. Eh, Jacques's teaching me Frog, y'know.

Norma What for?

Norma stays in the kitchen, we see her moving from one side to the other every now and again, very busy. She is not really listening to Mary. A lot of the time Mary is taking the piss.

Mary It's mainly so I can understand what he's saying on the phone, in case he's doing any dodgy deals. But we're gonna go to France for a holiday. I'm dead excited. We were gonna go to the south, y'know Cannes and Monte Carlo, but he reckons the police will still be looking for him there. So we're going to Paris. He keeps going on about staying in a git, although you pronounce it shite for some reason. Y'know what it is? One of these shites. Well, I'll tell yer. It's some cottage in the middle of a field (*she gets out a bottle of Sarsons Vinegar and applies it like suntan lotion*) and the deal is the people who normally live there are on holiday or they've died the week before. Well, if he thinks I'm sleeping in someone else's bed, he can go jump. What if they come back from holiday and we're in the middle of the Lovers' Guide? Or they haven't taken the corpse away, and you have to sleep next to some French stiff? I've told him. I want en-suite everything. En-suite bath. En-suite bog. En-suite bidet. En-suite Eiffel. En-suite hunchbacks. En-suite Lambrusco. The lot. So anyway we're gonna stay in some dead posh hotel in the French part of Paris. I did wanna fly but it's cheaper by coach and it only takes eighteen hours. Have you ever heard about the mile-high club, eh? Well, I'll tell y'. You become a member by having sex in the toilets on a plane. I don't know how they know, y'know, the people who run the club. I think maybe you get a certificate off the air hostesses. Anyway, 'cause we're going by luxury coach and y'know they have luxury toilets on them. Well, we're gonna start the foot-high club. Oh, it should be lovely. I was just gonna get a one-way ticket but he wants to stay 'ere. And I wanna stay over there. It's funny how I always go for foreigners. Are you listening?

Norma Yeah, yeah, that should be lovely, France, yeah. I wouldn't mind going to Anglesey again.

Mary Eh, take it easy, girl. You don't want to be too adventurous. I'm determined to get a good colour on 'ere. This'll probably be the only heat we get all year.

Norma comes out of the kitchen carrying a paint-splattered wallpapering table. She puts it under Gwen's window. She comes in and out, putting plates and food on it and talking to Mary at the same time.

Have you seen me sun-tan lotion? (*She holds up the vinegar.*) I didn't have time to get some new stuff this morning and it costs a bomb anyway. So I made me own. Baby Oil, fake tan and a bit of Fairy. I didn't have anything to put it in, and I found this (*bottle*). It lets just the right amount out. And I remember Jacques saying that all the Frogs put vinegar on their skin to get a tan, anyway, and it had a bit left in it. I had to spray a bit of Charlie in, though, to get rid of the smell.

Norma Mary, I'd go careful with that – y' don't want skin cancer.

Norma sets out paper plates and cutlery on the table. Steven comes out; he is going to tell his mum what he saw.

Mary I need to look good, 'cause the tartier I look the more tips I get in the pub. By the time I'm on me last legs I won't need to look like a slag. You don't need orange skin when you're delivering meals-on-wheels, do yer?

Steven walks up to Norma.

Steven Mum . . .

Norma is busy rushing about and listening to Mary. She sees Steven but just pats him on the head and carries on with what she is doing.

Mary (*looking up at the sky and about to put her sunglasses down*) I hope Max Wall hasn't let his pigeons out today. You know what they're like. I'll tell yer, Nor, if one of them even farts on me I'll be over there. They shit on me and I'll shit on him. Hiya, Steven, you all right?

Steven (*meaning, no I'm not*) Yeah. (*He looks at his mother.*)

Norma Isn't there anything good on the telly?

Steven No.

Mary What's our Gary and Rory up to?

Steven They've gone to have caterpillar races at Rory's house.

Mary Why didn't you go with them?

Steven (*having had enough of the questions, he moods inside*) 'Cause I didn't want to.

Mary Is he all right?

Norma I think the burglary has scared him a bit, I'll have a chat with him later when the party's over. Oh, my God, me sausage rolls. (*She runs inside and brings out a massive bag of frozen sausage rolls. She reads the instructions.*) Cook from frozen for . . . they'll take for ever. Oh, me scones are in the oven. Right, (*throwing them to Mary*) sit on them for me.

Mary Cheers. (*She slowly lowers herself on to them, the cold being a bit of a shock.*) God, sitting on these reminds me of that bloke from Barclays I went out with; y'know, frigid Fred. Are you sure you got enough 'ere, three hundred economy sausage rolls? How many people have y' got coming?

Norma is back inside, she doesn't answer.

Well, there's me, you and Gwen, that's three. There's your Tommy, my Jacques, our Gary and his mate Rory, that's seven. There's your Lizzie and Steven. Is Joseph coming?

Norma (*pops her head out*) Yeah. I've told him he's coming or else. If he's not here later I said I'd go round to his bedsit and drag him over 'ere. Our Steven'll be pleased to see him 'cause he hasn't been round for about a week. I've told Steven, though, there's to be no playing tricks on anyone, you know what those two are like when they get together.

Mary Yeah, tell me about it. Auntie Vye's still blind in one eye after that christening.

Norma I'm sure they'll behave. It'll be nice to have all the family back together again and I haven't had a good chat with him for ages.

Mary Well, let's just hope he's cut down on those pot noodles, he smelt like he had an alien up his arse the last time I saw him. Anyway, where was I? So that's all your three kids, that makes it ten. I think that's it. Oh, I forgot me mother, that's eleven.

Norma We'd better phone her and make sure she's coming. Knowing my luck she'll be going ice skating again and these butties'll go to waste. Will you phone her? (*bringing out the phone*) Ee are, love. Ask her what time she's coming over. I reckon about two's best. Don't tell her about the break in, y'know what she's like.

Mary She'll be off down the self-defence classes again. (*She picks up the receiver.*)

Norma Don't remind her it's her birthday, she'll only get confused.

Mary puts receiver back down.

But, then again, ask her if she knows what day it is.

Mary picks it back up.

Tell her I'll come over and pick her up. No, I'm not going to have enough time.

Mary puts it back down.

Tell her our Steven'll come and pick her up.

Mary picks it back up.

Mary Do you wanna do it?

Norma No, no, I've got to . . . Ooh, I'd better put these on. (*She picks up sausage rolls and goes back inside kitchen.*)

Mary Ee are (*Putting on a posh voice*) Hello, Mrs Pearl Malone? . . . Y' what? . . . What d'you want your loft insulating in this weather for? (*getting annoyed with her*) I know you were in the war . . . Mother, it's me, Mary, your daughter . . . No, I don't work for the Council . . . (*defeated*) OK, yes, I do then . . . Listen, can you come over to Norma's later? (*to Norma*) She's got to see that young doctor, so she'll come about one (*to Pearl*) Steven . . . your grandson will escort you over here . . . Do you know what day it is today? . . . National Arthritis Day? . . . well, we'll see you later then, Mother . . . Yeah . . . bye . . . Mother . . . bye (*Puts phone down.*) Au revoir. Is this party going to be worth the grief?

Norma (*coming out of the kitchen and standing in the doorway*) Yes, of course it is. Just to see her face when we finally give her her war medal. I mean, all this food's very nice but it'll all mean nothing compared to how happy she'll be when she sees it.

Mary Well, let's hope she'll shut up about the war now. I feel as if I was there. And about me dad. (*imitating Pearl*) 'Why did he get his medals while I never got mine?'

Norma Come on, Mary, she has waited long enough.

Mary Don't I know it.

Norma Eh, she'll be able to put it in that glass case with me dad's ones now.

Mary I bet you she wears it for a bit, I can see her preening herself, showing it off down the Co-op.

Norma She might as well, it's something to be proud of and it'll make all the hassle of getting it worthwhile. (*coming outside and putting some food on the table*) God, a medal for being a cook.

Mary (*eating crisps*) Well, I can tell y' now, *you* won't be getting one. If you ask nicely you can have a bag of crisps.

Norma I wonder what she's going to see the doctor about?

Mary She'll be fine. I know she's seventy but I reckon she'll be wind-surfing long after we've gone.

Norma She fancies Dr Matthews, doesn't she?

Mary No, he's younger than me. He is fit, though, isn't he, eh? I'll tell yer, he's got lovely hands. Whenever I have a big argument with Jacques, I pop down to see him and tell him I've got a lump. And he has a good feel.

Norma You're not serious?

Mary (*laughing*) You think that's bad. Y'know Annie Cragg from the pub. Y'know, Jughead, the one with the big ears and the small mams. She's had three smears off him in one month.

Norma No.

Mary They call her Internal Annie at the pub.

Norma Oh, that's awful. Anyway, shush. We don't want Desmond Tutu hearing next door, he'll have a heart attack.

Mary Eh, I'd better watch he's not perving out of his window. Is he still Mr Crimewatch?

Norma Yeah, if he's not running the church he's marching up and down like one of the Gestapo.

Mary Maybe he saw something last night?

Norma Oh, he's next to useless. If he'd seen anything he'd have been round here like a shot with his magnifying glass.

Mary He's just a nosy bastard.

Norma You're not wrong there.

Mary Ooh, a cloud. (*getting up*) Right, d'you want a hand while the sun's gone in?

Norma Yeah, can you butter some of these cheese sandwiches?

Mary (*in kitchen*) Yeah. (*looking round*) Eh, I've got a chance to try out some of me French, ee are: 'Quelle de marg.'

Norma Ooh, that's great. What does it mean?

Mary Well, what am I looking for? Eh? Quelle de marg? Where is the marg?

Norma It's next to the bread bin there. Where's it gone?

Mary It's all right, girl, it's here.

Norma (*getting angry*) Not the bloody margarine, Steven's family allowance book, I keep it in the bread bin. The bastards have taken that as well. (*coming outside*) How did they know to look there? Why can't we just have normal thieves who steal your video and your tiara. No, we have to get bloody wierdos who nick your chicken legs and root through your bread bin.

Mary Don't worry, you can get another book.

Norma Yeah, it takes for ever and in the meantime the

scumbags will be dressing up as me and cashing it, won't they? And I won't get any more bloody money.

Mary Sod them all. Let's just try and get through today first, shall we, and tomorrow I'll come down the Soc with yer and give them the screaming abdabs.

The telephone rings. Norma goes over to it on the grass and answers it. She listens and looks disgusted.

Norma Christ Almighty, that's all we need, a bloody heavy breather.

Mary (*takes phone*) Give it 'ere. (*listens*) . . . Jacques, what have I told you about phoning me here . . . Oh, stop it, you sound like an asthmatic . . . (*to Norma who is back in the kitchen*) He's in me bedroom trying on me clothes again . . . (*to Jacques*) If you ladder my tights I'll kill yer . . . I don't care what you're doing with a kiwi fruit . . . I am not phoning an ambulance if you choke yerself again. (*She slams the phone down.*) Soft get. (*She goes back over to the kitchen.*) Right, where was I? What d'yer want doing?

Norma (*going back outside and putting stuff on the table*) Can you make those cheese and onion butties for me?

Mary Yeah, OK. Are these for Lizzie? Is she still a vegetable?

Norma Yeah, three years it is now. Not one scrap of meat. Except for that time when me Mum thought chicken wasn't meat. I don't know what she thought it was, though.

Mary What were y' saying about her being upset? (*She comes to the door and listens while nibbling on a large piece of Cheddar cheese.*)

Norma Oh, Mary, I'm really worried about her. I don't

know where to begin. She's been acting really odd. She's still in bed now. She comes in in the middle of the night or first thing in the morning, usually crying and it's straight in the shower. Then she's asleep half the day. She says she's been watching videos and talking at Kelly's or Maria's, and that she has to have a shower 'cause of all the pollution in the air. Y' know what she's like. The thing is, I can tell when she's lying. (*short pause*) And then there's the money. All of a sudden she's splashing money about like there's no tomorrow. Her income support hasn't gone up, I've checked. She says it's money she's lent to people and they're paying her back. But tell me when she's had enough money in the past to become a self-made loan shark? She bought us this lovely gâteau from Marks's the other day. But whenever I ask her what's going on she just starts wingeing. Nearly three weeks it is now, of this palaver. I don't know what to do. If it carries on much longer she'll end up like our Gwen. (*to window, Gwen is not at the window*) You all right in there, love? (*to Mary*) Something's got to be done. If only so we've got enough hot water for showers in the morning.

Mary I wouldn't like to say what's going on there, Nor.

Norma I worry she's going to do something stupid.

Mary Is it that bad? Is it knives in the bath time?

Norma Y' wha'?

Mary Heard it all before. Hide the knives, the paracetamol, the plug off the kettle. Anything she might do herself . . .

Norma What are you going on about? Y' can't joke about things like this, this is serious.

Mary She wants to stop being silly and just get on with it.

Norma Everyone's not as tough as you, y'know.

Mary (*no reaction*) I'll tell you what. I'll ask her what's going on. She might tell me, she does confide in me sometimes. (*She goes back inside.*)

Norma Does she? Since when?

Tommy comes out the door.

Tommy I'm into town to sign on.

Norma You will be back for the party, won't y'?

Tommy Yes.

Norma If you see a trail of chicken legs, follow it.

Tommy You be Hansel, I'll be Gretel.

Norma Eh, remember to get that money off Father Barry, for doing his fence. He said he'd have it today.

Tommy Yeah, I won't forget.

Norma goes back inside and Tommy makes his way down the garden. As Tommy opens the gate Joseph rushes in and they almost bump into each other. There is a slight pause before they speak.

All right.

Joseph Hiya.

Tommy Have y' come for the chicken legs?

Joseph (*unnerved*) What?

Tommy (*tapping Joseph's stomach*) To get some proper food inside y'.

Joseph Oh yeah. Are you not staying?

Tommy No, I've got a book-signing session in town.

Joseph I've already done me autograph this week.

Tommy Good to see you're following in your father's footsteps. I can safely say I've taught you everything I know.

Joseph (*getting carried away*) Our Lizzie's keeping up the family tradition as well.

Tommy (*enjoying it*) I'm gonna get our Ste some pens for Christmas so he can get in training.

Norma comes out and puts some food on the table.

Norma (*to Tommy*) Are you still here?

Tommy No, this is a hologram. Tommy left an hour ago. (*He leaves.*)

Norma All right, love? (*She goes up to Joseph and hugs him, he is embarrassed.*)

Joseph Hiya, mum.

Norma How are y'?

Joseph Oh, fine, fine.

Mary (*poking her head out of the kitchen door*) Hiya, shitface.

Joseph Hiya, Auntie Mary.

Norma You look like you've lost a bit of weight, and you could do with a haircut.

Joseph Yeah, I suppose so.

Norma (*remembering*) I'm so glad you're here. You won't believe what happened 'ere last night. We only got broken into.

Joseph Yeah?

Norma Yeah, they got in through there.

She indicates the window. Joseph goes over and looks at it.

The new video, your brother's family allowance book and for some reason a load of chicken legs.

Joseph (*waiting for her to mention the medal, turning round*) Is that all they took?

Norma It's enough, isn't it? Did you want them to take more?

Joseph No, it's just . . . you're lucky they didn't take more . . .

Norma We've got nothing else for them to take, unless they wanted two thousand sausage rolls. Anyway, I'm trying to forget about it now and make the most of today. D'yer want a drink?

Joseph (*thinking*) Er . . . Yeah . . . I'll . . .

Norma Aye, I'll tell you what, you haven't seen your nan's medal, have yer? I'll just go and get it . . .

Joseph (*now realizing that she doesn't know it's been taken. Trying to stop her*). No, no, it doesn't matter, I'll . . . I'll just have that drink, please, Mum.

Norma I'll get you that in a minute, let me just show you it. (*Too late, she's gone inside.*)

Joseph looks round the garden in the hope of finding some means of escape. He looks into Gwen's window but can't really see, so he goes right up to the glass and cups his hands round his eyes. Gwen suddenly appears and makes him jump with fright.

Joseph Oh . . . hiya, Auntie Gwen, it's only me, Joseph.

He starts to panic and decides that he'll run off. He starts to make his way up the path, Mary comes to the kitchen door, with a big knife in her hand, crying.

Mary Me eyes, I can't stop crying.

Joseph turns round, shocked that she's crying, and gets tangled in some of the washing.

You don't wanna chop some onions for me, do yer? (*She goes back inside.*)

Joseph gets nearer to the gate when we hear Norma scream from inside.

Norma (*shouting*) No, Gwen, I'm all right, don't worry, it's just . . . nothing . . .

She runs out into the garden, runs in front of Gwen's window. Gwen appears, so she moves to the right so Gwen can't see her. Joseph stops dead in his tracks. Norma is close to hysterical.

God, I have to hide in me own garden. What's happening to us? Why us, eh?

Mary comes to the back door, to see what's going on.

(*to Mary*) Go and see if Gwen's OK, tell her nothing's wrong.

Mary What's the story?

Norma It's gone. No medal, no party, no nothing. It's over.

Mary Yer wha'? Have you looked properly?

Norma Of course I have. Go and check on her.

Mary goes inside. Norma and Joseph are left alone in the garden. Norma looks up to the sky. Joseph is frozen.

The bastards, who do they think they are? (*She turns round and starts to fix the washing.*) All we need now is a bit of rain. (*She bursts into tears. She stays with her back to us and holds out one arm to Joseph.*) Come here, son.

He goes to move but is glued to the spot. He eventually walks towards her very slowly. He embraces her. She gives him a big hug and she talks holding on to him.

Guess what?

He is speechless.

They took it, one tiny little piece of brass with its fancy little ribbon. Gone. They probably didn't even give it a second thought, just saw it sitting there on the fire, thought, 'I can get a couple of quid for that' and slipped it into their greasy little pocket. I feel as if I just went inside and they'd robbed everything I own. All me little bits and bobs, every memento, it's all just teared out and destroyed.

Joseph (*slight pause*) Come on, it's not that bad.

Norma You don't realize, do yer? (*pulling away from him and facing him*) Y' start with nothing round here and each day y' try to get a bit more. I don't want a lot, all I did want was one day where we could all get together, y'know, have a laugh and give me mother what she's been waiting so long for. No, that was too much to ask from the little gets round 'ere. They're like vultures, I'm sure they can smell a little bit of pleasure, they can sniff out a video no problem, but they must be getting advanced when they sense something which would have made me mother so happy. Never mind what it would have done for us. Well, they'll have some carcasses to feast on soon, your dad's nearly on his way and our Gwen and Lizzie don't look as if they'll last the pace. (*looking up to the sky*) I can feel them circling overhead. Our Mary was wrong, it's not pigeons she's got to worry about getting her. We might as well quit while we've still got the strength. (*She sits down on a chair she brought out earlier.*)

Pause.

Joseph I . . . I . . . I don't know what to say. (*He kneels in front of her.*)

Norma There's nothing *to* say. There's nothing we can do about it and we're stuck here. As long as we can try and keep a bit of dignity and not stoop to their level, we'll survive. (*She laughs.*) Dignity! With snot dribbling down me face. (*She blows her nose with the tissue from her sleeve and then wipes her face with the tea towel tucked into her apron.*) You don't know anyone who'd do this sort of thing do y'?

Joseph Naah.

Norma stares at him as he becomes very uncomfortable, and again looks for a means of escape.

Norma (*starting to get upset again*) The little shits. They're probably the same age as you, son, why would they do this?

Joseph I've no idea.

Norma What about those scallies who went to your school? You could find out for me . . .

Lizzie appears at the door in her dressing gown. She looks very tired.

Lizzie (*rubbing her eyes*) What's going on? What's all the noise?

Norma (*to Joseph*) You tell her.

Joseph We . . . er . . . got broken into last night.

Mary appears behind Lizzie's shoulder.

And the video and stuff was taken, and . . . erm . . . me mum's just found that me nan's war medal's gone as well.

Lizzie No.

Mary Aren't they mean? Just let me get my hands on them.

Joseph stares into space.

Norma So we might as well forget about the party.

Lizzie Oh, there's no point in giving up now.

Mary Too bloody right. After all the work I've put in today, it'd be a waste. It's still me mother's seventieth birthday, we've got that to celebrate.

Norma It won't be the same.

Mary Well, we'll make it the same. Come on, if the Kellys can't have a good party, well, it's the end of civilization as we know it.

Lizzie I'll just put some clothes on and go down the shops to get some goodies. (*She runs inside.*)

Norma That's all we need, her spending her dodgy money.

Mary We've gotta have a bash, 'cause I told Gwen in there that you were so excited about it you were crying with happiness.

Norma What are we gonna tell her about the medal?

Mary Oh, I'm sure you can think of some way of blaming our Gary for it.

Norma And what about me mother, what do we tell her?

Mary I know it's no consolation, but she didn't know she was getting it, did she, so it won't harm her, will it?

Norma It's not gonna stop her wanting it.

Mary We'll just have to try and get her another one, start all over again.

Norma Back to square one, it's like building a bloody sandcastle in quicksand.

Mary You never know, we might get the stuff back.

Norma Get real. It'll already be out the country, the medal'll be on some market stall in Marrakech by now.

Lizzie comes back, dressed but still looking shattered.

Lizzie Right, we're having this party and I'm not gonna hear another word said against it. I thought I could get me nan some flowers.

Mary That's a nice thought, love.

Joseph (*jumping up*) I'll come with yer. Give y' a hand.

Norma (*taking hold of his hand*) Thanks for looking after me, love.

Joseph That's OK. (*He's in a real hurry to get out.*)

Lizzie (*going over to the table and looking at the food that's out*) Have you done me some vegetarian stuff, mum?

Norma Yeah, cheese and egg.

Lizzie I thought I'd get some of those dip things as well.

Mary Ooh yeah, we can act all posh.

Lizzie I'll get a couple of bottles of Liebfrau and some beer for you (*Joseph*) and me dad. D'you want anything else?

Mary Have we got any Vimto?

Joseph is now at the gate.

Norma No, I didn't think we'd need it.

Mary (*going into her bag*) Well, look what I nicked from work. (*A bottle of vodka with the label on upside down,* *from a pub. Norma disapproves because it's stolen. To Norma)* It's me mum's birthday, she's gonna get her favourite drink at least. A double V. I've got the vodka, will you get the Vimto?

Lizzie Yeah.

Norma Have you got enough money?

Lizzie Yeah, plenty.

Norma and Mary look at each other.

See yer in a minute. (*To Joseph as they leave*) What's the hurry?

Norma See what I mean about splashing the money about? Where does a young girl like that get so much money from, eh?

Mary Don't worry, I'll find out. Come on, I know it's hard but let's try and enjoy ourselves.

Norma If I knew who'd done this. If I had just had them 'ere, I'd . . .

Mary Don't think like that, 'cause it's not gonna happen. It wouldn't be anyone we know. Right, it's party time, OK?

Norma (*unenthusiastic*) Yeah, party time. (*She goes back into the kitchen.*) These sausage rolls are done.

Mary (*as the sun comes out*) Oh, me friend's put his little hat back on. (*She looks to the left*) The pervy little bastard. Saint Desmond's got a pair of binoculars. Well, I'll give him something to fuckin' look at. (*She rips off her bikini top and waggles her boobs at him.*) Wooeeaah, is this what you wanted to see? He looks like he's seen a ghost. That surprised yer, didn't it? (*pleased with herself*) Eh, Nor, he's (*from pleasure to shock*) clutching at his chest.

What's he doing? He's sliding down the inside of the window. What's he playing at? He's trying to scare me by pretending he's ill.

Norma brings out two massive pyramids of sausage rolls and puts them on the end of the table.

Norma Leave him alone, will yer. He's probably just a bit shocked. He is ancient, he's as old as Bidston Hill. Will you put yourself away. (*She goes back inside.*)

Mary I hope he's not sick.

Norma He'll be fine. He'll be down the church later with his sister doing his Pope bit, showing the altar boys when to ring their bells. (*She comes out with two more massive piles of sausage rolls and puts them on the other end of the table, leaving a space in the middle.*)

Mary (*seeing the sausage rolls*) Piss me! Wasn't your Joseph gonna be an altar boy?

Norma Yeah, but Desmond used to scare him. I think he takes his boys quite seriously and he didn't like our Joseph messing about. Our Steven talks to him, but y'know what he's like, he'd have a good chat with Dr Crippen if he bumped into him. (*She goes back inside.*)

Mary Your Joseph doesn't seem himself.

Norma Mmm, I think the break in was a bit of a shock for him. Although he doesn't live 'ere I think he still sees this as his real home in a way. He'll be fine once he sees our Steven and they start playing about.

She brings out the final two piles. Mary is speechless and just looks at them. Norma puts them in the space in the middle.

Sausage rolls. (*She goes back inside and makes more sandwiches.*)

*Steven comes out of the house with two washing-up
liquid bottles full of water.*

Mary What are you up to?

Steven I was just gonna have a squeezy bottle fight in the
street.

Norma (*from inside*) Put yourself away, Mary. You're not
in Corfu now.

Mary I'm just getting a bit of a bronzy. (*to Steven*) I'm
sure you've seen it all before, anyway.

*He smiles. She puts her bikini top back on. Steven
stands by the table trying to fix the lids on the bottles.*

Norma (*at the door*) Oh yeah, Steven, while I remember, I
had Mrs Skinner round here yesterday. She doesn't want
you doing the Grand National through her front garden
any more, and I think that goes for the rest of the street.
You could do yourself some serious damage jumping over
those fences and hedges. So tell Gary and Rory as well,
yeah? (*She goes back inside.*)

Mary (*picking up one of the bottles and going over to
Steven, whispering*) Eh, Steve, listen, the next time you go
through her garden pull a moony through the kitchen
window. She was trying to spoil our fun when we were
your age. That's what me and your mum used to do.

*Norma listens at the kitchen window, Mary pretends to
be serious.*

So be told. (*She starts playing about with the water,
squirting Steven.*) Come on, you can't get me.

*They squirt at each other. Mary runs in front of the
table, Steven soaks her and the table gets a bit wet.
Norma comes running out brandishing the bread knife
she has been cutting food with.*

Norma (*screaming, over the top, she points with the knife.*) Will youse two get away from that table and stop messing about. If there's even a speck of water on that tablecloth . . . Look at that, y've got all me food wet, have you two got no common sense, you don't spray water around just anywhere, can you just stop arsing about. (*Going to go inside*) I've had enough of this.

Mary and Steven stand shocked, Norma has the knife pointing out.

Mary Er, excuse me, what's wrong with you, eh? (*to Steven*) D'yer wanna go outside and play, go on, write your name on the road with the water, and watch it dry.

Steven goes up to the gate, he watches his mum for a second, and goes out, squirting on the ground.

We were only playing with water, y'know. What has got into you?

Norma I don't know. I just want everything to be perfect.

Mary What are you doing with that?

Norma (*she doesn't even realize she's got the knife in her hand*) What am I doing? (*dazed*) Oh, I was just making some more sandwiches. I'd better get back inside . . .

Mary Will you just calm down, everything's gonna be fine. Just look at the weather, I'll tell yer, I don't think we could have picked a better day if we tried.

Norma OK, OK, everything's under control. Right, most of the food's sorted. The scones just need browning a bit. I'll just get some chairs. Our Gwen can blow some balloons up for us. (*She goes inside, speaking to Gwen.*) Ee are, love, will you blow these up. Just put them out the window when you've done them.

Norma brings some chairs out, Gwen posts balloons

*through the broken window. An ambulance siren is
heard briefly, as if it is outside the theatre.*

Mary Shall we have a drop of vodka, to get us in the
mood, eh, Nor?

Norma We could have a sip. Shall we have it with orange?

Mary Naah, we don't want to deaden the taste. (*She fills
two glasses.*)

Norma Bloody hell, go easy.

Mary Right, knock 'em back.

Norma Yer wha?

Mary After three. Three. (*Knocks it back in one. Sirens
come back louder.*) Ooh, that's got me warmed up a bit.

Norma Aren't you hot enough? Ooh, the veins in me head
are all sticking out now. Is that an ambulance?

Mary It sounds as if it's coming here.

Norma Steven! (*She runs out, unsteadily.*)

Mary (*sitting back down and lighting a fag*) D'yer wanna
see if they've come for our Gary?

Norma (*at the gate, watching*) It's gonna stop here, no, it's
gone next door. It's at Desmond's. They're going inside.

Mary Maybe he saw something to do with the burglary.

Norma I think he'd call the police not the paramedics.
That was quick. They're coming out again. He's on a
stretcher. Jesus, he looks like death.

Mary (*showing no emotion apart from annoyance at the
inconvenience of neighbours dying next door*) Oh, great.

*Smoke starts coming out of the kitchen. The balloons
are piling up outside Gwen's window.*

Norma His sister's with him, that nun. What's she doing? She's got her rosary beads out. She looks a bit upset.

Mary (*now really pissed off*) Fuckin' great. He's dead, isn't he?

Norma What's our Steven doing? Come away from there. She's giving him something.

Mary I've killed Bishop Desmond Tutu.

Norma They're going now. The ambulance is driving away.

Mary Thanks for the running commentary. We've got fuckin' Kate Adie in the garden.

Norma Come here, Steven.

Steven appears from the left.

Steven Look, Mum, Desmond's sister gave me his binoculars. She doesn't think he'll need them any more. They're smart, aren't they?

Norma What happened?

Steven She was saying something about finding him upstairs out cold with the binoculars in his hand. She reckons he'd been watching a bird.

Mary I'm no fuckin' bird.

Steven She thinks he's had a heart attack. He's had two before.

Mary He's had two before? Well, he was a time bomb waiting to go off. I've done him a favour. He could have been all on his own. This way he had his family round him.

Norma Aah, that's awful, the poor man.

Mary Serves him right for perving.

Norma Mary! Have a bit of respect, will yer, it looks like he's just died.

Mary Oh, give over, what d'yer want us to do? Scrap the party and have a wake? We've got enough bloody sausage rolls.

Norma I'll say a prayer for him.

Mary You do that.

Steven Can I go up to Biddie Hill with these (*binoculars*), Mum?

Norma You can go tomorrow, son. You'd better go and pick your nan up soon.

Steven stands at the bottom of the garden looking at the gate through his new binoculars. Norma notices the smoke from the kitchen.

Bless us and save us. (*She runs to the kitchen, through the sea of coloured balloons.*) Oh, buggery. (*She throws the flaming pan out of the kitchen door on to the path. She watches the flames.*) Vodka time. (*Pours herself a vodka.*)

Mary (*not moving*) You all right there, Nor?

Norma Yeah, yeah, fine, smashing.

Lizzie comes through the gate with bags of shopping.

Lizzie What was the ambulance doing here?

Mary Oh, it was just one of the neighbours dying.

Lizzie (*lost*) Right.

Norma Let's put some deccos up. (*Seeing all the balloons, she shouts through the glass*) I think we've got enough balloons now, Gwen, love. Thanks. (*She stands on a chair and hangs up a Happy Birthday banner above Gwen's window.*)

Lizzie I've got all the stuff. I got the flowers, wine, dips, beer and the Vimto.

Norma A little spending spree, eh? Where's Joseph?

Lizzie He's just coming with the rest of the stuff. He just stopped for a minute. Y'know, he's been really doing my head in. I don't know what's wrong with him but I had this big argument with him in the middle of Kwik Save.

Norma What about?

Lizzie He said he wasn't gonna come back, something about not being able to handle it, I dunno.

Norma (*to Mary*) I told yer, he's upset about the break in, he's just a big softie really.

Lizzie goes inside. Joseph walks in. Steven looks at him through the binoculars, from his feet upwards. He gets to his face and takes the binoculars off. He stares at Joseph. Joseph smiles and stretches out his hand to put it on Steven's head.

Joseph Hiya, Ste, you all ri . . .

Steven Mum, I'm going to get me nan.

Norma OK son. Don't tell her anything, though. We want it to be a big surprise.

Steven runs out.

Joseph What's wrong with him?

Norma (*to Joseph*) Come inside, son, I'll get you a can from the fridge, you deserve it. (*They both go inside.*)

Mary Let's get this karaoke machine set up. (*She puts it below Gwen's window and passes the flex through the broken window.*) Gwen, can you plug this in for me, girl. (*She tries out the microphone.*) Testing—one—two—three—

testing. Two fat ladies, eighty-eight. Major's den, number ten. (*speaking and not singing*) You make me feel like dancing, gonna dance the night away. That'll do. (*She nicks some food off the table.*)

Lizzie comes out with the stuff she has just bought and fills up the table.

Lizzie Mary, look at this for when me nan comes. We'll just have a little rehearsal. (*shouting in to Gwen*) When I say, yeah? Now.

Gwen holds up two pieces of card, one with seven on and one with nought. We can see them through the net curtain.

Good, eh?

Mary She should've be an ice skating judge.

Joseph and Norma come outside.

Norma I think we're all ready. It's the time, they should be here soon.

Lizzie (*to Gwen*) You can put them down now, Gwen. I'll give you a shout when.

Mary I'll just see if they're coming. (*She goes to the gate.*)

Norma Oh, my God, the washing. (*She runs over and starts to take it down.*) It's dirtier than when it went in. Mmm, what a lovely aroma, burnt bloody scones.

Mary Shit, they're coming.

Norma (*to Lizzie and Joseph*) Give me a hand.

They all get a bit panicked. Lizzie helps taking stuff off the line and Joseph holds the basket. Mary puts her blanket/sun lounger away and puts the tent under the table. Lizzie picks up the tray of burnt scones, which is still a bit hot and puts them on top of the washing basket, takes it off Joseph and goes inside.

Lizzie, the washing.

Joseph gives everyone a party popper each.

Are we all ready?

Lizzie Eee are, you take these. (*She hands Joseph the flowers.*) Take your apron off, Mother.

Norma (*as she does*) OK. When they walk in we all shout 'Surprise'. Yeah?

They all go quiet.

Joseph Shush.

The gate opens.

Lizzie Now, Gwen.

All shout 'Surprise' at different times and they let off their party poppers. Gwen puts her numbers up. Pavlov starts barking. Two plain-clothes policemen walk in: middle-aged **D. I. Tower** *and younger* **P. C. Buck**. *The two police are dumbfounded.*

Mary Who the fuck are you?

Norma Mary! Pavlov! (*She throws a sausage roll over the fence, and the dog stops barking.*) Can I help you?

Mary If you're Jehovah's Witnesses we're past salvation.

D. I. Tower (*not happy with their reception*) If you don't mind, we're the police. (*Everyone freezes, especially Joseph. They show their IDs. He speaks to them with no respect and is quite menacing.*) Are you having some sort of a celebration?

Norma Yes, it's my mother's seventieth birthday.

D. I. Tower (*sinister sarcasm*) How nice.

Lizzie (*defensive*) Well, what d'you want?

D. I. Tower You did phone us, didn't you?

Norma Oh, yeah.

D. I. Tower You have had burglary, haven't you?

Norma Yeah.

D. I. Tower That doesn't really matter, because we were on our way over here, anyway.

Norma Yeah?

Mary What for?

D. I. Tower I think we'd better go somewhere a bit more private. (*to P. C. Buck*) D'you want to go and do some dusting inside, Trevor.

Norma (*trying to lighten the atmosphere*) D'you wanna do a bit of hoovering while you're there?

D. I. Tower (*not amused*) Let's just go inside, shall we.

All three go inside. Pause.

Lizzie You can put the numbers down now, Gwen.

Mary I wonder why they were coming. (*She looks across to Desmond's garden.*) They could be coming to see any of us. I hope youse two haven't been misbehavin'. (*She looks at Lizzie especially.*)

Lizzie covers her eyes and Joseph looks to the sky.

Shit. (*She runs over to the phone and dials quickly.*) So you haven't suffocated yourself this time. Put some Savlon on it and if it doesn't go down we'll go to hospital . . . I certainly will not kiss it better . . . (*getting annoyed with him*) Shut up a minute, you can't come over, the place is crawling with police . . . Au revoir. (*She puts phone down and goes back to watch at the gate*) Jacques. (*going back over to the gate*) I'll go see if the other two are coming. My eyesight must be going when I can't even recognize me own mother.

Norma comes back out.

Norma I've left them to it.

Joseph What did they want?

Norma We've got to keep this to ourselves, but they want to use our bedroom to watch a house across the street.

Mary What for?

Norma All they said is that they'd had a tip-off about the burglaries that have been going on. And that they'll be using our house for (*posh voice*) surveillance purposes.

Mary And you're gonna let them?

Norma Yeah, why not?

Mary Well, I wouldn't let them in my house without a warrant. They'll be snooping around, sniffing through yer knickers drawer, the lot.

Norma We might as well help them out, they'd never catch anyone if we all took your attitude. And, anyway, we've got nothing to hide, have we? (*Pause. No one answers.*) Have we?

Lizzie Why our house?

Norma They said it's the one with the best view.

Joseph (*still anxious*) So they'll be here all day?

Norma Yeah. What's wrong with youse lot? You'd think you hadn't seen police before?

Mary Eh, I'll tell yer what, that young one, what did he call him? Trevor? He was fit, him. He had lovely hands, did you see his thumbs? I wonder whose house they're watching.

Norma They wouldn't say.

Mary I bet you it's the Clarkes' place. I always knew they were tea-leafs. Ever since their Nancy stole me compass in primary school. (*looking out*) They're coming. It's definitely them, I can see me mother skipping.

Norma Right, we won't shout surprise this time, we don't wanna start Pavlov off again.

Mary And we don't want any more old people dying of shock.

Norma Are we ready? (*to Lizzie*) Where's your father?

Lizzie Now.

> *Gwen puts her numbers up, upside down.* **Pearl** *and* Steven *enter through the gate. She is talking and totally oblivious to what's going on.*

Pearl Any road, the upshot of it was, they couldn't save his legs but his feet were fine. So now he's got wooden legs and real feet. Ooh, I'm going to miss the beginning, that's you, that is, keeping me talking.

> *She walks through the garden and into the house, not noticing anyone. They all stand frozen and stunned. We hear the theme tune to* The Young Doctors, *very loud.*

Mary Is this what she meant about seeing the young doctor?

> *Norma puts her hands over her eyes and Steven stands on the path by the gate watching Joseph. Gwen keeps the numbers up.*

Act Two

SCENE ONE

Complete darkness, except for a spotlight on Mary's head and shoulders as she sings on the karaoke machine. She is wearing her bikini top and sarong. It should seem as if she is singing in a club, with a glitterball and maybe even a sparkly background. She sings 'Crazy' by Patsy Cline. She sings with lots of guts and tries to imitate Patsy. She accentuates the end of each word in true pub singer style. She acts like it is her final farewell performance at Wembley Stadium, giving it everything she's got, and not the back garden of a house in Birkenhead. At the end of the first verse the lights come up to reveal that we are still in the garden with the sun still shining brightly. Mary continues singing the whole of the song. Pearl is ballroom dancing with Stephen. Lizzie is asleep on a sleeping bag on the grass. Norma and Joseph are sitting next to each other, Norma drinking a glass of wine. Gwen is dancing on her own in her window.

Most of the food has been eaten except for the sausage rolls, the banner is wonky, there are empty cans, paper plates and serviettes on the grass. The telephone has been taken inside. The bouquet of flowers is in a bucket by the back door. There are a couple of empty bottles of wine on the table, but everything else is as before.

Half way through the song Norma gets Joseph up to dance. He resists but eventually gives in. After dancing for a while and just before the song finishes both trip over Lizzie lying across the garden and wake her up. They trip over on to each other, laughing a lot. Lizzie tries to get back to sleep. The song finishes. Everyone claps. Pavlov starts barking, so Norma throws it a sausage roll.

Pearl You must have some Dionne Warwick, Mary.

Mary No, I'm sorry, Mother, I've only got Country and Western hits, The Beatles and songs from *Grease*. We might as well have one more classic. (*She presses 'play', and the intro to 'Stand by your Man' plays.*)

Joseph 'Ere we go again.

Mary imitates Tammy Wynette. She sings the first two lines, but after 'giving all your love to just one man', the tape gets chewed. Everyone goes 'Aah'.

Pearl (*now quite tipsy*) Thank fuck.

Mary and **Norma** (*both horrified*) Mother!

Pearl Well, how can you have a party without any Dionne?

Mary We should be able to fix it. (*She takes the tape out and all its insides are hanging out and caught in the machine.*) Maybe not.

Norma Er, I think it's time for the cake. (*She goes inside to get it.*)

Mary Ooh, yeah.

Pearl It'd better not have seventy bloody candles on it.

Mary Don't worry, the fire brigade are standing by. (*to Norma*) Come on, girl, we're losing valuable drinking time 'ere.

Norma I'm coming, I'm coming. (*She comes out with a big iced cake with two candles on it, a seven and a nought. Everyone goes 'Aah'.*) Come on, everybody, let's sing.

They sing 'Happy Birthday'. Joseph kicks Lizzie to wake her up, she sits up and sings, really pissed off. Mary on the microphone sings 'bread and butter in the gutter' version. Pearl sings the loudest to herself. Everyone else is very non-committal. When it comes to the 'dear . . .' bit everyone sings different things: Mum, Mother, Nan, Grandma, Pearl. Pearl hesitates but then blows the candles out and everyone claps. Pavlov barks.

Mary (*to Pavlov*) Shurrup.

Norma throws another sausage roll over the fence and the barking stops. Lizzie lies back down and goes to sleep again.

Norma Ee are, cut the cake. (*She hands Pearl a bread knife.*)

Pearl I hope it's not fruit cake, I can't stand fruit cake.

Norma (*taking the cake and knife inside*) We'll cut the cake later.

Steven watches Joseph drinking for a minute and then follows Norma inside. Joseph stands at the table drinking from a can and eating. He nervously looks up to the bedroom window where the police are watching. We hear the chimes of an ice-cream van coming down the street. It is playing 'Raindrops Keep Falling on my Head' too fast and very plinky-plonky, the music sometimes slows down and speeds up for no apparent reason.

Pearl (*to Joseph*) Joseph, let's go into the inner sanctum and you tell me and your lovely Auntie Gwen how school's going? (*noticing the ice-cream van*) Ooh, would you like an ice cream, son?

Joseph Naah, I'm all right with me can. Our Steven might want one.

Pearl Ee are, go get him one. (*She takes out her purse and hands him ten pence. He waits for more but it's not coming.*) Is that enough?

Joseph Er, ten pee? Yeah?

Mary (*going into her bag*) Ee are, here's a pound, kid.

Ice-cream van music stops.

Joseph (*as he goes out the gate*) No one else want anything?

Mary (*sarcastic*) Naah, we've got all this lovely food. Mum, ee are, have a double V.

Pearl Ooh, yes, smashing.

Mary Are you having a good time, Mother?

Pearl Yes, love, it's lovely. The weather's glorious. Did you decide to do this when you saw it was going to be a lovely day?

Mary Well, we picked today, because we thought we'd have your birthday party *on the day* of your seventieth birthday.

Pearl (*really casual*) Maybe I should have told you I'm seventy-four.

Mary Why?

Pearl 'Cause that's how old I am.

Mary Yer wha'?

Pearl I think it was because I liked being twenty-three so much and I stuck with it a bit too long. Y' get past fifty and you lose count, years just pass you by like bank holidays. I realized I was seventy-four when all the D-Day stuff began, because one thing I do know is I wasn't fifteen when the war started.

Pause. Mary looks at her mother.

If only I was fifteen. Is Elizabeth tired over there?

Mary I think she must be, she's deado.

Pearl She's what?

Mary I mean she's exhausted.

Pearl Aah. That'll be with working down the Council. She's going to insulate my roof later in the week.

Mary No, mother, that was me.

Pearl What does Elizabeth do?

Mary She hasn't really got a job at the moment.

Pearl Aah. A lovely looking girl like that. She should be able to waltz into anything.

Mary Yeah, I'm sure she could earn a lot of money. (*now certain in her own mind as to what she thinks Lizzie does*) She is pretty and that's just what some people like.

Pearl Aah.

Mary stares at Lizzie transfixed, she then goes over to the table and helps herself to some food and pours herself another glass of wine, as Joseph comes back in with a big ice cream with red sauce on it.

Ooh, isn't that lovely, I'll give him a shout. (*She goes to the door, she's forgotten his name. She remembers.*) Steven, come out 'ere, son.

He comes out.

Look what . . . er . . . your brother's got y'. Let's get some games started.

She goes in. Mary has her back to them and is unaware of the atmosphere between the two brothers.

Joseph I got yer favourite. Raspberry ripple, strawberry sauce and hundreds and thousands.

Steven says nothing.

Ee are.

Pause. Steven says nothing.

Take it.

Steven I don't want your ice cream.

Joseph It's not off me, it's off me nan.

Steven Mary, will you tell me mum I've gone over to Rory's for a bit.

Mary (*turning round*) OK, son, don't be too long, though, your mum'll get worried. Eh, and if you see any bad men you know what to do. Send em round 'ere.

Steven runs out. Joseph stands there, he looks at Mary.

He didn't want it?

Joseph says nothing. He looks at the ice cream for a second and walks inside, confused and dejected. Mary looks over to Lizzie and is about to try and wake her up. P. C. Buck enters through the gate carrying a couple of bags of chips. He talks to Mary.

P. C. Buck He wanted chips.

Mary (*just being friendly*) There's plenty of food here if you're hungry, and there'll be birthday cake doing the rounds soon.

P. C. Buck I'm sure if he wants anything he'll send me down for some more.

Mary Have you seen any masked bandits yet?

P. C. Buck Naah, only the couple across the road bonking in their back garden. I don't think they thought people would be watching with binoculars.

Mary (*adjusting her bikini top*) You should've been 'ere earlier.

P. C. Buck You what?

Mary Nothing. Number seventeen, was it?

P. C. Buck Yeah.

Mary Those bloody Tremarcos. Let's just hope her husband comes back from the rigs early and catches them changing ends.

P. C. Buck Oh, right. It's funny what people get up to when it's hot.

    Pause.

Mary (*flirting, going in for the kill*) I love the heat.

P. C. Buck Mmmm.

Mary I suppose I should really put me dress back on.

P. C. Buck Y' might as well make the most of it while it's out. And it's nice to have something else to look at from up there. (*Embarrassed at what he's just said, he tries to get out of it, but only makes it worse.*) You've really caught the sun on your back.

Mary Could you do me some more lotion? (*She goes to her bag to pick up her lotion.*)

P. C. Buck (*trying to escape*) Don't wanna let the chips go cold.

Mary (*getting him back*) D'yer want some vinegar? (*She shows him the Sarsons lotion.*)

P. C. Buck (*taking it*) Oh yeah. (*He goes to go inside but comes back.*) I don't like it but old Sherlock has his chips swimming in it. Ta, see yer later. (*He goes in.*)

Mary Bye.

*Mary watches Lizzie asleep on the blanket. She lights a
cigarette and then goes down to her and tries to wake
her up.*

Liz, Lizzie, come on, wake up.

Lizzie (*as she bolts up*) What is it? What's happening?

Mary Don't worry, girl, it's only me. You don't wanna
sleep all day, you won't be able to sleep tonight and you're
missing all the fun. You missed me singing.

Lizzie I didn't, I've just been dozing, but I thought me nan
would have me up dancing if I moved. Though I would
have been up and running if you'd've got any further with
'Stand by your Man'.

Mary Cheers.

Lizzie It's just I'm not Country and Western's biggest fan.
But then again, who is?

Mary Are you tired, Lizzie?

Lizzie A bit. I didn't get much sleep last night.

Mary Why not? What were you doing?

Lizzie Nothing. I was round at Kelly's watching a video.

Mary Yeah? What did you watch?

Lizzie (*defensive*) Is this an exam? A-level Life?

Mary I'm just interested. You might've seen a good vid I
haven't seen.

Lizzie Oh, it was some dead old film, it had that Richard
Gere in it.

Mary Ooh, I love him. He's gorgeous, isn't he?

Lizzie He's a bit old.

Mary Was it *An Officer and a Gentleman* or *Pretty Woman*?

Lizzie Yeah, one of them.

Mary Ah, both of them had me crying me eyes out. Especially in that army one, that bit when his mate tops himself in the bath. Sad or wha'?

Lizzie Oh . . . yeah . . . I was still crying when I got back 'ere.

Mary Yeah? Your mum said you'd been a bit upset recently.

Lizzie Oh really? Is that what this is all about? Have you been sent over to interrogate me? What's she been saying to y'?

Mary Only that you've been a bit moody recently.

Lizzie Moody. That's what I'm supposed to be. I am still a teenager, y'know.

Mary Yeah, but you're usually so positive, so happy.

Lizzie There's not exactly much to celebrate around 'ere, is there? That's if you don't count me nan's party. Though she hasn't got a clue what's going on. I'm sure she thinks it's our Steven's seventh birthday.

Mary Maybe you're not getting enough vitamins. I'll tell yer, you need some meat inside you. Maybe I should rephrase that?

Lizzie I've been a vegetarian for three years now and it's done me no harm.

Mary You can tell me what's bothering yer, y'know. It often helps to confide in someone, get it out in the open, come out of the cupboard. There is something bugging yer, isn't there?

Lizzie I don't wanna talk about it.

Mary Yer know what they say, a problem shared is a problem . . . what was that? It's something to do with fractions.

Lizzie A problem shared is a problem, full stop. It doesn't make it go away by telling someone else.

Mary Come on, it's not like *Oprah*, there's me 'ere. Yer don't have to tell me, girl, but it's obvious you're bottling something up.

Lizzie (*becoming upset and initially angry*) I just got fed up with having no money. Counting the days till I got me next dole. I only wanted to go out with me mates and get pissed. Wanted to buy meself some new clothes and get me hair cut properly. Y'know me mum goes on about having dignity and morals, and, yeah, great, but can't I have them and not look like a dog twenty-four hours a day? It looks like you've got to scrap one to have the other. Y'know I only wanted a bit of cash so I could buy me mum and dad stuff as well, cheer them up a bit. Oh, I dunno. It all sounds stupid now. I sound like some snotty little teenager. I want, I want, I want. But why shouldn't I be able to have a few nice things? Everyone else does, have I done something wrong? Is there some special rule that people on this estate are always gonna get crapped on? Maybe I should check me birth certificate again, Elizabeth Pearl Kelly, born Birkenhead, 5th October 1975, shit life guaranteed. No refunds available. (*She is now very upset.*)

Mary Aye, love, come on, there's no need to get upset.

Lizzie It's just . . . just, I can't stand meself for what I've been doing. I've supposedly got all these big principles, but

I get a sniff of money and it's out the window. As if I don't give a toss any more, but I still do, there's no other way though . . .

Pearl (*running out into the garden*) Who's up for a game of musical statues? (*She stands still like a statue, but wobbles.*)

Norma appears in the kitchen at the sink. She looks out at what's going on.

Mary (*had enough of Pearl, wanting to get rid of her*) We've got no music, Mother, the tape player's broke.

Pearl Aah. What a shame.

Mary See if Joseph can fix the old record player, inside.

Pearl Ooh, yeah, then we could have some proper music. (*She dances her way back in, singing 'Say a Little Prayer' by Dionne Warwick.*)

Mary Oh, my God.

Lizzie is still crying. She puts her cigarette out.

Aah, kid, let me get you some tissues.

She goes to the kitchen door, Norma is coming out. She stops her.

Norma What's wrong with Lizzie? She looks awful.

Mary You told me to talk to her and that's what I'm doing.

Norma If I wanted her to cry I would've spoken to her meself. I seem to have no difficulty in getting her to break down. Let me talk to her.

Norma tries to get across, Mary stops her.

Mary She'll tell you whatever she wants later, pass me some tissues.

Norma What's up with her? What's she been saying?

Mary I'd tell yer, but you'll only start screaming.

Norma I won't, I'm totally calm. I haven't had that much to drink. Tell me.

Mary No. She'll tell yer in her own good time.

Norma Tell me or I'll find out meself.

Mary Don't go mad, but I think she's been working down Corporation Road.

Norma (*stern*) No. No. No daughter of mine is a prostitute. Let me . . . (*trying to get past*)

Mary Well, we'll never find out the truth if you go over there and start a slanging match.

Norma But . . .

Mary Norma, go inside.

Norma I . . .

Mary Pass me the tissues. (*new tactic to get rid of her*) Listen, go inside and go through her coat pockets . . .

Norma You've gone mad.

Mary Just do it to see if she's anything in there she may be hiding. Just in case she won't tell me.

Norma I can't go . . .

Mary Just do it, it'll be better in the long run.

> *Norma passes Mary a large roll of kitchen roll and quietly goes back inside. Mary goes back to Lizzie.*

Ee are, girl, come on, dry your eyes.

Lizzie (*seeing the size of the kitchen roll, joking*) Are you taking the piss?

Mary You don't have to tell me if you don't want to. 'Cause I know what you've been up to.

Lizzie You do?

Mary Yeah. It wasn't hard to work it out.

Lizzie I feel so dirty. When I come home I stink. I have to scrub meself clean.

Mary So this is where you've been getting all the money from.

Lizzie (*composed*) Yeah. Before I started doing it I was desperate, I could see no way out and I just wanted to finish it. And now, OK, I'm happier I've got money, I can do some of the things I wanted to, everything should be hunkydory. But I hate meself for what I'm doin' and I'm sure I'm making meself ill.

Mary You are being careful, aren't you?

Lizzie Well, as careful as you can be. (*pause*) Y'see. I'm still not happy and it doesn't look like I ever will be, is there any point to all this?

Mary Y' don't wanna think like that.

Lizzie Why not? There isn't any point in goin' on.

Mary I know how yer feel, but . . .

Lizzie Don't say that, you haven't a clue how I feel.

Mary Yeah, I have. I know it sounds corny but I know what it's like to have had enough, to think that it's all downhill, that's there's no hope . . .

Lizzie (*half shouting*) You're just saying that to shut me up.

Mary (*quite aggressive, with no self-pity*) And why would I wanna lie? Eh? Don't you dare tell me I don't know. (*She*

153

shows Lizzie her left arm which has a scar on it.) Look, doesn't that say I understand?

Lizzie You did that in work on some broken glasses.

Mary (*still angry*) Oh, yeah, that's what I told yers all, didn't I? Oh, sure, I did it on some broken glass, but it wasn't in the pub and it wasn't an accident. Naah, I smashed the glass in me kitchen, on the draining board to be precise. And I wasn't carrying too many and tripped over a barstool, no. I held out me arm, (*she demonstrates*) and I just stabbed it in a couple of times. Our Gary found me, phoned the ambulance and sorted me all out. What did I tell him? Oh that was it, I tripped over a loose carpet tile as I was getting a glass of water. An alibi for every occasion, that's me. It's becoming a little hobby. I was gonna tell yer' mum but she's got enough on her plate as it is.

Lizzie Why did yer do it?

Mary Good question. (*pause*) I should have been singing 'Tears of a Clown' not 'Crazy'. I . . .

> *Norma makes retching noises from the kitchen and throws Lizzie's coat out on to the path. Norma comes out to Lizzie.*

Norma What have you got in your pocket?

Lizzie Have you been going through my pockets?

Mary Obviously.

Lizzie What's going on here? What is this, Strangeways?

Norma Oh, don't be daft, Elizabeth, we know what you've been up to. What is in your pocket?

Lizzie I don't know.

Mary (*picking up the coat*) May I?

154

Lizzie What have I got to lose, Mary?

Mary searches through one pocket. Nothing. She goes through the other one.

Mary Ee aar. What's this? (*She pulls out a veiny testicle.*) Jesus wept. (*She holds it in the palm of her hand.*)

Lizzie What does it look like, it's a testicle.

Norma Mary, Mother of God.

Mary (*meaning 'oh my God'*) Bollocks! (*She throws the testicle on to the grass.*)

Lizzie OK, bollocks, then. (*dead casual*) I have to use their proper name once I've cut them off.

Norma Oh, my dear God. (*She sits down by the table.*)

Mary What have you been doing to them?

Lizzie What d'you mean?

Mary What I say.

Lizzie Well, killing them, of course.

Norma Jesus, Mary and Joseph.

Mary Keep your voice down. Starsky and Hutch are up there.

Lizzie What's your problem? What else am I supposed to do with them?

Norma Where did I go wrong?

Mary How can you be so casual about it?

Lizzie I'm not happy about it, y'know. I was crying for a reason.

Norma We'll all be crying soon.

Mary What d'you do with them once you've killed them?

Lizzie We just put them in a . . .

Mary We? There's a few of you?

Lizzie Yeah, there's more who do it during the day but there's quite a few of us at night.

Mary Are you in some sort of cult or something?

Norma How can you do this?

Lizzie Don't make me feel worse than I already do. Oh yeah, how do you think I feel, eh? Big strict vegetarian working nights in an abattoir. If the people at Chicken's Lib found out. The number of times I've thrown up . . .

Norma and Mary look at each other.

Norma What did you say?

Lizzie It makes me sick.

Mary Before that.

Lizzie What is this? D'yer want me to be happy working in an abattoir?

Norma (*realizing*) You've been killing animals?

Lizzie Yeah?

Mary Like sheep and pigs and cows and . . .

Lizzie OK, don't rub it in.

Mary and Norma look at each other and start laughing hysterically. They cannot stop.

What's so bloody funny? Stop laughing. What happened to all the concern?

Norma Oh, give over. Don't get upset, love. You should be proud.

Lizzie Proud?

Norma Yeah, proud. Y've got a job, you found it off your own back. Not many people could do that.

Mary (*still laughing, and picking up the testicle and putting it into a half-filled wine glass*) I'll tell yer, I bet it wasn't advertised in the *Liverpool Echo*, eh, love?

Lizzie Will youse two stop going on about it. I don't want to talk about it any more.

Norma Fair enough.

Mary (*trying to stop laughing*) Shall we finish off that bottle of Liebfrau, eh?

Lizzie Yes.

    Norma takes the glass with the testicle in it.

Norma I'll just get some clean glasses. (*She goes inside.*)

    Lizzie sniffles.

Mary It's all right now. Don't y' feel better?

    Lizzie says nothing.

Listen, we would've found out anyway, that's what secrets are like. They always come out and y' can't hide anything from your mum.

Lizzie Yeah. But where do I go from here? What's next?

Mary (*she thinks and tries to be considering but fails*) Dewhursts?

    Lizzie gives her a look.

We'll sort y' out, we'll find the silver lining. (*pause*) Eh, you wouldn't be able to get us some cheap chops, would yer? (*She starts giggling again.*)

Lizzie Mary!

Mary Joke! Sorry.

Norma comes back out with three odd glasses: a pint tankard, a wine glass and a tumbler.

Norma 'Ere we go. (*She pours the final dregs into the glasses.*)

Mary Cheers.

All drink.

Lizzie What did you think I'd been doing?

Mary and Norma look at each other, their mouths full of wine, trying not to burst out laughing.

Mary Er, animal rights.

Lizzie Yeah?

Norma hides behind Mary as she tries not to laugh.

Mary Yeah, animal rights. Yes, we thought you'd been, er, setting free, y'know, doing things with beavers in the middle of the night. But in fact you were doing the exact opposite.

Lizzie Oh . . .

Mary Nice wine.

Norma No more secrets, eh?

Mary (*unable to keep her laughter in any more*) I think I'll leave youse two alone for a minute, I'll just go and see how our Gwen and me mum are. (*She goes inside.*)

Norma Shall we play some party games in a minute?

Lizzie Like what?

Norma Gwen's made some parcels for Pass the Parcel.

Lizzie Where are they?

Norma and **Lizzie** (*at same time*) In a brown cardboard box under the stairs.

Norma Oh, you know?

Lizzie Yeah, me nan was looking for the toilet, she found them all and thought they were birthday presents. She couldn't work out why there were twenty wrappers on a fun-sized Mars Bar.

Norma Oh well, that's the end of that, then. (*She finishes her drink and goes over to the table.*) I think I'll try a double V. D'you want one?

Lizzie I'll have a small one.

Norma starts making them in the glasses they've just used.

Mary was going on about triple Vs before, but I'm not that keen on vinegar.

Norma Have you seen your father yet?

Lizzie I haven't seen me dad all day, I haven't spoken to our Ste either.

Norma Him and Joseph are very quiet, I think they're up to something. I always can tell when those two are scheming.

Lizzie Are they ever not playing tricks on each other? And it always ends in disaster. I still have nightmares that they got me and not me Auntie Vye.

Norma Oh you never know, maybe they're planning a nice surprise for your nan, to try and make up for the medal going. (*still making the drink*) Lizzie?

Lizzie Yeah.

Norma What was that thing doing in your pocket?

Lizzie Oh, that'll be Carmen getting me back.

Norma (*handing the drink over*) What for?

Lizzie I put a willy in her welly.

Norma (*frowns, then cracks a smile.*) Cheers. (*Drink.*)

They drink.

Lizzie Oooh, that's gross.

Norma Oh it's got a nice kick to it.

Tommy comes through the gate, quite cheerful. He has a brown cardboard box in his hand.

About time too. Thought you'd pop in, did yer? You've missed a good bash, Tom. Hasn't he, Liz?

Lizzie (*sarcastic*) Yeah. Great.

Norma Eh, I've got some good news. Young Lizzie 'ere . . .

Lizzie Mum!

Norma Has found herself a job.

Tommy Yeah? Well done.

Norma She's working down at the abattoir . . .

Tommy I thought you were a vegetarian?

Lizzie I was. I mean, I am.

Tommy Well, I wouldn't eat meat if I had to kill it meself.

Lizzie I hate this house. (*She storms off inside.*)

Tommy What's wrong with her?

Norma I think it's the stress and strain of a new job. She's got her hands full there. She'll get the hang of it. What's that (*the box*)?

Tommy This is the end to all your, our worries. It'll stop any more burglaries.

Norma What is it? A machine gun?

Tommy No, an alarm, a burglar alarm.

Norma Where . . .

Tommy Don't worry, it's all above board.

Norma Is it knock off?

Tommy No, look, it's in its box.

Norma Let me see. (*She opens the box.*) Eh. Oh, yeah, this looks smart, it's even got instructions with it.

Tommy Yeah? Yeah.

Steven comes through the gate.

Norma Hiya, love.

Steven says nothing. He sits down on the grass at the front of the stage, facing the audience. He picks up the kitchen roll, tears off a piece and folds it into a flying bird during the next bit of dialogue. He is still wearing the binoculars around his neck. He puts them down next to him.

(*getting the instructions out*) Let's see. (*reading*) How to get the best out of your Breville Sandwich Toaster!

Tommy It must . . .

Norma Oh look, a recipe booklet as well. Mmm, cheese, tomato and Branston pickle or maybe banana and peanut butter. That's amazing, it not only protects yer house but cooks you up a light snack while you're there.

Tommy It's just been put in the wrong box.

Norma What d'you take me for? Where did you get this from?

Tommy It's kosher, Bitter Barnes said . . .

Norma Oh, yeah, Bitter Barnes. I should have known. He's as bent as a bottle of crisps.

Tommy No, love, he was with his wife and . . .

Norma Gladys Barnes. She's just as bad, she hasn't got a clue. She's a walking advert for Diazepam.

Tommy No, Norm . . .

Norma You know what I think. I don't want any dodgy stuff in my house. For a start, if this alarm has been nicked, it's not doing its job very well, is it? And even if it did work y'know that I don't want stolen stuff in there. Did y' see any of our stuff on display down the pub, did yer? Yeah, we could have cheap stuff. We could've had the house fitted out ages ago, chandeliers and bidets in every room. But no, 'cause we'd only be stealing from ourselves in the end. We'd be paying for everything twice. Just 'cause our neighbours are stealing from us, we don't have to do it back. We might as well get everyone in the street to open their doors and get a big conga going. In through the front door and out through the back. We take the stuff from one house and place it in the next . . .

Tommy Don't act stupid, Norma.

Norma I'm not the one who's being stupid.

Tommy Where does all these principles get us, eh? We deserve to have something, just once.

Norma Not this way, Tom. I can't. Take it back (*handing him the box*).

Tommy Take it back! It's not from Marks's, y'know. You can't have your money back if it's in its bag with a receipt.

Norma I don't care. Bitter Barnes will be able to sell it to some other mug.

Tommy Go on, just spit on me while I'm down.

Norma I can't be doing with this, Tom, not today.

Tommy Rightio. (*He goes to leave.*)

Norma Did you get that money off Father Barry?

Tommy (*holding up the box*) I'm gone. (*He leaves.*)

Norma stands watching Steven, who has finished making his bird and is now flying it about, pulling the bottom so the wings flap. Joseph stands in the doorway for a minute watching both of them, then comes out of the kitchen with a cup of tea.

Joseph Ee are, mum. Me Auntie Mary's just made it.

Norma Ta, love. Ooh, it's getting a bit cooler now. What are they all doing inside?

Joseph Me nan's playing Pin the Tail on the Donkey, but we haven't got a donkey so they're using one of our Lizzie's old Save the Whale posters. And instead of a tail they're using one of me Auntie Mary's hair extensions. So they've renamed it Pin the Wig on Moby Dick. Oh, and one of those policemen is in the toilet throwing up. He said his chips tasted a bit odd.

Norma I thought they got rid of all the cockroaches at the chippy?

Joseph Yeah, they did. The other copper's all right, though, so it must be something else.

Norma Did they eat any of our food?

Joseph I don't know. I don't think so.

Norma Oh good, 'cause that kwish was well past its sell-by date. I thought it was broccoli on top, but it turns out it's mould. Will you do me a favour, love?

Joseph Yeah, if I can.

Norma Go and have a word with our Steven, see if he's OK. I haven't heard a peep out of him all day.

Joseph Yeah, he's been well weird. He hasn't fallen out with Rory or Gary, has he?

Norma No, I don't think so.

They both watch Steven playing with his bird for a brief second.

I'll go and cut some cake and bring yer both some out. Ooh, the sun's starting to go in, I'd better put something a bit warmer on. (*She goes in.*)

The sun starts to go in. Joseph sits next to Steven. Steven tries to ignore him.

Joseph Did you just make that?

Steven Yeah.

Joseph Where did you learn to do that?

Steven Me nan got me an origami book last Christmas.

Joseph Are those binoculars me dad's?

Steven No.

Joseph Whose are they?

Steven Mine.

Joseph Where d'you get them from?

Steven Desmond from next door gave them to me.

Joseph Yeah? (*Silence.*) He was dead weird, him.

Steven No, he wasn't. He was just old.

Joseph They look just like me dad's old ones.

Steven Yeah, but you smashed them, didn't yer, dropping them down that hill when we were on holiday in Wales.

Joseph That wasn't me, that was our Lizzie. Don't you remember we had the binoculars and if you looked through them you could see the windmill on the top of Biddie Hill. And then we were watching those happy campers arsing about in the wind on top of that other hill. And that bloke's . . .

Joseph and Steven . . . wig blew off.

They both smile, Steven remembers and tries to be difficult again.

Joseph Then we climbed down the hill and *that's* when Lizzie broke the binoculars. I broke the torch. I had to use something to knock the tent pegs in, and it only needed a bit of Sellotape on it.

Steven Yeah, but it still doesn't work properly.

Joseph (*trying to make contact with Steven*) I used to love it in Wales. Playing frisbee with the dried cowpats, though our Lizzie always picked a fresh one. (*Pause, Joseph waits for a response.*) And going for big walks and if you got thirsty you could stop, have a drink from a stream, then move on. (*Pause, he waits, but no answer. He tries again.*) Eh, and all in the same tent, trying to get some sleep through me dad's snoring. That day we woke up and the field was full of cows, they must have thought he was a bull.

Short pause as Joseph waits for Steven to join in, as he has in the past.

Steven (*giving Joseph a chance to explain*) I was camping last night, out 'ere.

Joseph I know.

Steven How d'yer know?

Joseph Er . . . me mum must've said something. Y' should've gone to Wales instead, there's loads to see if you go camping there.

Steven There's things to see round 'ere as well.

Joseph Like wha'?

Steven Loads, there's loads to see if yer look for it.

Joseph (*saying, no there isn't*) Oh yeah?

Steven wants to say something but he can't. Pause.

Steven Y' can see . . . (*He changes the subject*). Well, just like you could see the windmill on the top of Biddie Hill from Wales, you can do it the other way round. (*He gets really animated and you can tell he's really thought about it.*) If you stand just beneath the windmill you can see right over to Wales, all the hills and trees like a big green quilt and if you turn round and face the other way you can see Liverpool, with all the big massive buildings piercing the sky. Y' can see them all, the cathedrals, the Liver Birds and the UFO Tower. But the thing is, you can't see the Dee or the Mersey in between. The water just disappears. It's like you could walk all the way from the city right over to Wales without anything stopping yer. And now I've got these (*the binoculars*) I'm going to go up to Biddie Hill and watch all the tiny people on one side and the little cotton-wool sheep on the other.

Joseph Mmm.

Short pause. Steven talks to Joseph as he normally

would and is more relaxed for a minute.

Steven I keep on asking me Mum if we can camp up there, but she won't let me.

Joseph She'll let you do it when you're older.

Steven That's what she said. But by the time I'm old enough they'll have built houses on it by then.

Joseph Why don't you get someone older to go with you. (*Meaning himself*)

Steven Our Gary's gonna ask me Auntie Mary, she might do it.

Joseph She'd wanna take one of her fellas with her.

Steven Yeah. I dunno. I did ask Father Barry, but he said he's too busy at the moment.

Joseph What did y' ask him for?

Steven 'Cause he came into school to tell us about church and stuff, and we were talking about what we thought heaven looked like. I told him I thought it was like Biddie Hill because you can see everything you want from there.

Joseph What do you mean 'everything you want'?

Steven Don't you remember me mum and dad used to want to live in Wales and when we went on walks we used to pick out the cottages we liked and look through the windows to choose the bedrooms we wanted.

Joseph Yeah. And our Lizzie used to always say she was gonna live in the loft.

Steven Well, that's what I want. I wanna live in Wales when I grow up. I'm gonna work over in Liverpool in the city centre during the week. And live in a little flat just by the cathedrals. And while I'm there, me mum and dad will live in my cottage over in Wales. Then at the weekend I'd go over to the cottage and we'd all go for walks and stuff. It's smart and I can see it all from the top of Biddie Hill.

Joseph Do me mum and dad know about this?

Steven No, it's gonna be a surprise, so don't tell them.

Joseph Don't worry, I won't. (*short pause*) I used to think like that when I was still working at Asda. I was gonna have one of those big massive old houses up in Oxton Village and we'd have parties every weekend. All me mates would come over and they could all stay the night.

Steven Y' could still do it.

Joseph Oh yeah, sure, in me dreams. They were dreams then and that's where they'll stay. D'yer know what I dream about now, eh? Going down the dole office to sign on and not seeing me dad and our Lizzie there. It's crap, isn't it?

Steven Father Barry was saying if you really believe in something and really wanna do it you can.

Joseph What does he know? I'd like to see him lose his job and have to sign on.

Steven It's not that bad.

Joseph Oh yeah, of course it isn't. Where've you been living all yer life? You tell me dad 'it's not the end of the world', 'mustn't grumble', 'that's life' and, oh yeah, 'if you don't laugh you'll cry' and all the other crap people come out with. You tell most of the people on this estate that. Why d'yer think everyone's so bloody miserable, eh? Why d'yer think people are beating each other up, burning down their own homes and robbing from anyone they meet, eh?

Silence. Pause. Steven builds up to asking about the burglary.

Steven Is that why y' did it?

Joseph Did what?

Steven You know.

Joseph I don't know what you're talking about.

Steven I heard yer, I saw yer. Last night. I was having a wee.

Joseph Y' what? Oh, is that what all the silent treatment was about? Have y', have y' told me mum?

Steven What d'you think?

Joseph You can't tell her.

Steven Why shouldn't I?

Joseph She'd go mad. You didn't see her when she found the medal had gone. She was hysterical.

Steven Well, what d'you expect? She's been preparing for this for ages. She's been going on about it since this time last year, saying that it'll be better than Christmas. She's not just gonna sit down and forget about it, is she?

Joseph How d'yer think I feel, eh? It's been like torture 'ere today.

Steven Don't try and make out you've have a hard time, no one made you do it. You chose to break in.

Joseph No, I didn't.

Steven Oh yeah?

Joseph You don't understand, d'yer?

Steven Of course I don't. Who would?

Joseph Well, let me explain. There is a reason.

Steven Go on, then.

Joseph But promise that you won't tell her or anyone, not even our Lizzie. 'Cause if you do that'll be it. I'll just go away, go to another part of the country. I've worked it all out.

Steven OK, yeah, I promise. If I wanted to tell anyone I could have well done it by now. (*slight pause*) Go on, me mum'll be out in a minute.

Joseph I owed this lad some money, not much like. Then I saw him one day and he said it was all right about the money, that I didn't owe him it any more. And that was it. So that was fine by me. But then these trainee thugs turn up and tell me that now I owe *them* the money, because this dickhead had 'transferred the debt'. Before I know it I owed them loads more. And they started sending these heavies round all the time, trying to scare the shit out of me. Which they did. Then the other day they came round, they couldn't find any money, so they smash me bedsit up as a 'warning'. I was so shit scared I didn't even leave the flat, so I was still there when they came round the next day with good news, *for them*. They'd found out that me mum had just bought the video.

Steven How?

Joseph She'd only gone and joined the video club over there (*points out of the gate*). Which they practically own. So they were gonna come round 'ere and rob this place, instead. I pleaded with them not to, but in the end we came to this agreement that I would break in, 'cause I knew where the stuff would be.

Steven You still didn't have to.

Joseph Oh, don't give me that shit. If I'd've let them come round 'ere, they wouldn't have just nicked stuff. That's not their style. Naah, when they do a place over they fuckin' destroy it. They rip everything up, shit on the carpet, piss on the settee. They don't give a toss. They even make loads of noise so that the people upstairs will hear them. So they can beat them up. For a laugh. For a buzz. Y'know me nan's friend from the bungalows, Mr O'Malley, the one who was knifed? That was them. They just don't fuckin' care.

Steven Yeah, but what was the money for in the first place, drugs?

Joseph If only. Don't be soft. It was only fifty quid, that's all I borrowed. And y' probably won't believe me. I don't care if you do or yer don't. But it was for a video for me bedsit.

Steven I didn't know you had a video.

Joseph I haven't. It got nicked, of course. I didn't tell me mum 'cause it was knock off and y'know what she's like.

Steven You don't need a video.

Joseph No one needs a video, but I wanted one. You want your cottage in Wales, I wanted a video. But everything has to come to an end. Usually sooner than later round 'ere, and it was gone. I still had to pay for it, though. So I end up stealing a video to pay for a stolen video that was stolen in the first place. It's mad, people don't bother using cash round 'ere any more. This must be the only estate with its own currency. Y' just pay for everything with videos. (*short pause*) And I still end up with nothing.

Steven And so does me mum and me nan. Why did y' steal me nan's medal as well?

Joseph I thought they might want it 'cause there was no cash, but I didn't need it.

Steven So what did yer do with it? Sell it? Where is it?

Joseph I didn't know what to do with it, so I've still . . .

Pearl comes out, they both stop dead.

Pearl Hiya, lads. I've had enough. I'm going to bring
Dionne over here to get the party going again. Shall we
have a game of Give Us a Clue when I get back? (*She goes
out the gate singing 'Anyone Who Had a Heart'.*)

Steven I thought I knew you. You're not the same person I
grew up with.

Joseph Who d'you think you are, eh? Don't go and have
some teenage temper tantrum on me. I thought you might
understand, y'know, see it from my point of view.

*Norma comes out carrying a square metal tray with
drinks and plates on it. She walks up behind them. She
goes to speak but Joseph is saying something, so she
stands there listening.*

How d'you think I feel, eh? How d'you think I felt
climbing through that (*he points*) window last night, eh,
breaking into me own mum and dad's house, I was scared,
too . . .

*His arm is still outstretched behind him and he realizes
that there is someone standing next to it. He looks and
sees Norma. She is just looking at him. She is not sure
whether it is a joke or not, but soon realizes.*

Norma Go on, give me the punch line. I said youse two
would be playing a joke, I hope this is it. Tell me it's a
joke, it's meant to be funny, yeah? (*She knows it's not. She
starts getting very angry, upset and aggressive.*) I want to
laugh. Come on, tell me it's a joke, tell me, I wanna hear
you say it's not real. Tell me, Joseph, speak to me.

He bows his head, which is as good as telling her.

Tell me, please tell me, go on tell me, tell me now.
(*shouting*) TELL ME!

*Norma throws the tray down in front of her. All the
things on it smash on the grass. Steven and Joseph both
jump up. Mary and Lizzie run to the kitchen door.
Norma lashes out and hits Joseph on the nose. She
keeps hitting him while screaming at him.*

Why? Tell me, tell me why? Come on, tell me. You
bastard, bastard, how dare you, how dare you.

*Mary runs over and pulls Norma away from him.
Norma stands staring, she holds back her tears. To
Mary.*

Get off me.

*She lets go. Joseph's nose dribbles blood. Norma stands
in the centre of the garden facing Joseph. Steven stands
next to Norma. Mary and Lizzie stand further down the
garden. Everyone is still.*

Mary What's going on 'ere? What's happened?

Norma Shall I tell them this time? You know our visitor in
the night? Well, the mystery's over. He's here. Yeah, it was
him, my own son.

Mary Nooo.

Norma Yeah. (*to Joseph*) That's right, isn't it? Stop me if I
go wrong, yeah? So y'know what you were saying about
the thieving bastards knowing what they wanted. Too
bloody right, they knew. I mean, he knew. Exactly what he
wanted and where it would be. Why didn't you use your
key, eh? It would have been much easier. You could've
done it during the day, when you came round for tea last
week. Did you have a good laugh, did yer? A good buzz?
Was the group of yer? I'll bet it was a scream. Not as
funny as seeing me crying earlier, eh? Did you feel good
inside, satisfied? That you'd got the desired result? Eh? Or
was it better watching us save for the video and chase

round to get me mother's medal? Is that why you moved out? I never could get a proper reason as to why you were moving. So this is it. You took your time though, didn't yer? What is it? A year and a half? I suppose you had to wait until the crucial moment, when you could do most damage. Well, I'll give you that, you couldn't have picked a better time. (*pause*) So why did yer do it? Are you on drugs?

Joseph shakes his head.

Are you sure? You must be on something. I can't even look at yer. Y' bastard.

Lizzie Mum!

Norma Don't you mum me. I've been up most nights soaking fuckin' chickpeas for you while you've been cutting up sheep. So keep out of it, m'lady. (*to Steven*) Don't you look at me either. You knew about this and you didn't tell me. Did you plan it together? Where did I go wrong, eh? (*to all three*) Why do I bother? Look at yers, all yer do is lie to me, I didn't bring yers up for this. What's happened to yer? (*to Steven*) And you've only just started. What do you wanna be when y' grow up? A murderer? A rapist? I'm sure one of these two'll show you the ropes.

Mary Come on, Norma, take it easy, we can sort this out.

Norma Sort this out? It's a bit late for that now, isn't it? (*to Joseph*) What I wanna know is, didn't yer think of anyone else? Like me and yer dad. Obviously not. And what about her in there, eh? (*She points to Gwen's window, Gwen is not there.*) I've lost count of the number of years it's been since she last went out. She really thinks the minute she walks out the door she'll get attacked again. Where would she hide if she knew the thing she's scared of had been in her own home? Eh? Where would she go then? Where would any of us go? And what about yer nan, eh? Did you get a bit of money for her medal, did yer? Eh? Eh?

Silence. Joseph goes through his pockets to get the medal out. Pearl comes back in with a record. He is distracted.

Pearl Oh, you've started playing without me. (*She looks at all of them.*) Is it a film? *The Good, the Bad and the Ugly?* (*She walks inside.*) I'm right, aren't I?

Norma (*grabbing Joseph's arms, which are straight down as his hands are in his pockets, stopping him from getting the medal out*) Haven't you got anything to say for yourself? I said I wanted a good chat with y', well, now's my chance. Come on, I'm sure you can try and lie your way out of it. We're all waiting. Come on, speak to me.

Joseph I . . . I can explain.

Norma Oh, there's some sort of explanation, is there? Fire away, I'm all ears, I can't wait to hear this.

Joseph (*after a long pause, shaking with fear*) I . . . (*He tries again.*) I . . .

'Do You Know the Way to San Jose' by Dionne Warwick comes on very loud, starting with the big drum beats. It is a bit scratched. Everyone is distracted. Joseph can't speak now. Norma stares at him. She takes a tissue from her sleeve, spits on it and wipes the blood from his nose, quite clinically. When she finishes that she looks at him, very upset. She then runs inside. Everyone else stands frozen. Joseph goes into his pockets and produces the medal, he holds it out in front of him and drops it on to the grass among the broken plates and glasses. The others look at him disgusted, not knowing what to do.

After a while and near the end of the song Norma

comes back to the kitchen door. She walks out, goes up to Joseph and holds out her arms to hug him. He initially thinks she's going to hit him again. He realizes she isn't and hugs her tightly. He and the rest of the family think she's forgiven him. She is in fact saying goodbye. After a while she tries to pull away but he doesn't want to let go. The two police now appear at the kitchen door, they watch and wait. Norma finally pulls herself away and moves up against the fence and gate. D. I. Tower signals to P. C. Buck to take hold of Joseph, which he does. Joseph and the rest of the family now realize what is happening. Joseph tries to resist being taken away and he looks towards Norma for an answer. She looks at him for a minute until it is too much and then she looks away. Joseph is led away out of the gate now very upset. Mary, Lizzie and Steven look towards Norma in disbelief at what she's done. Lizzie runs inside.

We hear the thumping drum beat of the end of the song and then the loud buzz of speakers still on. Everyone is frozen for a minute. All very tearful. There is a long pause in the silence as no one quite knows what to do. Mary goes up to Norma.

Mary Come on, Norma, let's go inside.

Norma is led inside by Mary. Steven stands still.

Pearl (*shouting from indoors*) Shall we have the other side?

'Walk On By' by Dionne Warwick plays very loud, right from the introduction. Steven listens to the music and thinks. He has a plan. He goes over and picks the medal up, looks at it for a minute and pins it to his T-shirt. He then picks up the binoculars and puts them round his neck. He picks up the torch. He picks up the rolled up tent and puts it under his arm. He stands by

where the tent was left.

Steven (*quietly at first, sort of to himself*) I'm going to Biddie Hill, Mum. (*He walks over to outside the kitchen door. He shouts inside.*) I'm going up to Biddie Hill. (*He dashes over to the gate, opens it, looks out and really shouts.*) Mother, I'm going to Biddie Hill.

He smiles. He looks towards Bidston Hill as the music swells as the violins come in at the end of the first chorus, he walks out through the gate. We catch a glimpse of Gwen and Pearl dancing in the window. The song continues playing. The sun begins to set.

Afterword

The Knocky is Michael Wynne's first play.

October 1993   Stepney Green Library. While supposedly researching for my final year college dissertation, I find myself reading leaflets about the London Buddhist Centre, the Docklands Seafood Fair and a poster inviting anyone to write a play for the Royal Court Young Writers' Festival. Seems like a good distraction from college, so I take up the invitation and phone up to take part in a writers' workshop. By accident, I become a member of the Young People's Theatre and before I know it I'm a Scouse pig in a play about homelessness.

November 1993   Phase One Workshop at the Young People's Theatre, Ladbroke Grove. I make it to the intended workshop which is run by Roxana Silbert, a theatre director. It is intended for young people who have not written before. We talk about the theatre we like . . . This doesn't last very long. We go on to do a number of writing exercises, this culminates in me telling the group fifteen things my grandma says. The idea is that we now go off and start writing a play. At this point, I haven't the faintest idea what to write about.

February 1994   Phase Two Workshop. A group of actors are assembled to work on the scenes we have written. I'm the only one who hasn't written anything. I have thought about a plot and some characters and I try to explain it to everyone but it all becomes very confusing. The deadline for finished plays is May.

April 1994 I've realized that my dissertation has to be handed in the week before my exams start and the final date for play submissions is mid-exam. I decide to try and write both over the four-week Easter holiday, giving me two weeks for each. I set up camp in the college computer room and start typing.

Early May 1994 Give the play, at this point called *The Garden*, to Roxana Silbert for some initial feedback. Hand in my dissertation (which partly covers John Smith's arguments for a national minimum wage) on 5 May 1994 – the day he dies.

Late May 1994 Meet up with Roxana Silbert. She is enthusiastic and suggests improvements. Am spurred on by this, but I have my exams to do. I hand it in as it is and forget about it.

Early June 1994 Finish my exams, leave college and get a job in a restaurant.

Late June 1994 Get my degree results – I've done all right. The play is shortlisted for a weekend of workshops. Dig it out and work on a rewrite.

July 1994 Phase Three Workshop. Ten plays shortlisted. Each one is read by a group of actors and then discussed. Everyone seems very supportive. Do a bit of fine tuning and send it back in. It is now called *The Knocky* as in 'knock off'.

13 October 1994 First performance of *The Knocky* at the Royal Court Theatre Upstairs.

Michael Wynne
May 1995

ESSEX GIRLS

Rebecca Prichard

Josephine Jacobie

Josephine Jacobie
Born on a Monday
seduced on Tuesday
feller left Wednesday
they put her out Thursday
she get a job Friday
the money done Saturday
she cry all Sunday
the baby born Monday
What you think she call the baby?
Josephine Jacobie

Kendel Hippolyte

Characters

Diane
Kelly
Hayley
Kim, aged 17, a young single mother, Kelly's sister
Karen, aged 17, Kim's friend
Mark, (as voice off)

Act One: The school toilets of a comprehensive school, Essex, early summer.

Act Two: A council flat in Tilbury, Essex, still early summer.

Essex Girls was first performed at the Royal Court Theatre Upstairs in association with the Royal National Theatre Studio on 18 November 1994 with the following cast:

Diane Nicola Stapleton
Kelly Melissa Wilks
Hayley Emma Owen Smith
Kim Siobhan Hayes
Karen Faith Flint
Mark Jonathan McGuinness

Director Roxana Silbert

Act One: The Party

The girls' toilet of a comprehensive school, Essex. Graffiti is scrawled on the walls like a massacre: 'Slag', 'Hope', 'Bitch', 'Die, not, not, fade away', 'Jo is a slag', 'This schools an arsehole', 'Slow poke, Good poke' 'Eat me', 'Dog' and, in smaller writing: 'Sarah 'n' Dave, 2 gether 4 ever Never 2 part'. Hearts are drawn, some drawn then crossed over. Also there are conversations, traded insults, feuds and statements of pain: 'He said he loved me he lied, why me?' etc. The toilet is at war, but the room itself is ignorant of this as everything is still and silent. A sign hangs on one of the toilet cubicle doors – OUT OF ORDER. Fade up to bright. Enter Hayley, Kelly *and* Diane, *dressed in customized school uniform.*

Diane Stinks in 'ere.

Kelly Dark.

Hayley (*pushing on the toilet door*) Dyin' for a piss. (*It's locked.*) Oi, 'ooz in there?

Kelly (*knocking as well*) C'mon. 'Urry up.

Diane (*who has walked front stage to look into the mirror/audience*) God, I look a dog.

Hayley 'Ooz in there? Diane, you going French?

Diane (*scrunching her hair in the mirror/audience*) Dunno. Are you, Kelly?

Kelly Nah.

Hayley That new teacher's got a lump on his head, inee.

185

Kelly Oh, yeah, looks like he's got an ankle on his head.

Hayley They've all got bits in the wrong places, teachers.

Diane Like spare parts.

Kelly Yeah, I just had English. He's weird, as well. He's got no bum.

Hayley (*to the toilet*) C'mon, 'urry up.

Diane God, I look a dog. (*She finishes with the mirror.*)

Hayley They're all weird.

Kelly goes into a cubicle.

Diane I swear, if ever I end up lookin' like any of the teachers in this school . . . I ain't even gonna think about it, 'cos I won't.

Kelly (*from inside the cubicle*) Eeeuuurrgh!

Diane What?

Kelly There's a big fat tammy in 'ere.

Diane and Hayley rush into the cubicle to Kelly.

Diane Euuurgh!

Hayley Euuurgh. It's still alive.

Kelly It's a miscarriage.

They emerge from the toilet.

Diane That's your lunch.

Hayley That's your future family.

Kelly Ain't goin' in there.

Hayley I wonder whose it is?

Diane Didn't you see the name tag?

Hayley Said it's yours.

Diane Oh yeah, forgot.

Kelly Maybe we should take it to lost property.

Diane Who's in that one?

Kelly Iss locked.

Hayley Who's in that one?

Kelly Says 'Out of Order'.

Diane Thas out of order that iss 'Out of Order'.

Kelly Ho-ho.

Diane Whose in that one?

Kelly Iss locked.

Hayley I know, but who's in there?

Kelly Dunno.

Hayley (*to the locked cubicle*) 'Urry up, what ya doin'?

Kelly She's holding a seance wiv herself.

Diane Yoo-hooo.

Kelly Yoo-hooo, it's for yoo-hooo.

Hayley (*knocking on the locked cubicle*) Scuseme, you've got a phone call.

Kelly Who from?

Hayley God.

Diane She says God ain't allowed in the Ladies toilet.

Hayley He can see everywhere.

Kelly E's a perv.

*They give up on the locked cubicle. Diane lights a
cigarette. They pass it between them.*

Diane We just done sex education in Biology.

Kelly Who wiv?

Diane Mrs Lord.

Kelly Mrs Lord?!

Hayley (*indignant*) She ain't ever had sex, I bet.

Diane We walked in, right, and we all had to turn to page
41 and there was this big willy drawn there, looked like it
had horns. Then Mrs Lord wrote this word 'SEX' on the
board and we had to call out everything to do with it.

Kelly What did you call out?

Diane Aids. Then Paul Davies arksed Mrs Lord if she's a
virgin.

Kelly What did she say?

Diane She goes 'See me afterwards'.

Hayley And everyone went . . .

Kelly and Hayley Woah!

Hayley Can you imagine her ever having sex?

Diane Paul Davies arksed her what the proper name for
willy is, he reckons his Dad always calls his Duncan.

Hayley Eurgh.

Kelly (*thoughtfully*) My uncle's called Duncan.

Diane He arksed her for some condoms.

Hayley Him? What for?

Diane Reckons he's gonna put the sex back into Essex.

Hayley Fat chance he's got.

Kelly Can you imagine Mrs Lord ever having sex, though?

Hayley I bet when she opens her legs bats fly out.

Diane Eurgh.

Kelly I wonder when she does it.

Diane On Fridays.

Hayley In the still of night.

Kelly When there's a full moon.

Hayley Like howling.

Diane I wonder if she gives him marks out of ten.

Hayley (*imitating Mrs Lord's voice and pointing to the ceiling*) Aim high, aim for the sky.

Diane I bet she keeps naming all the parts of the body.

Kelly I bet her husband can't shut her up.

Hayley I bet he goes, 'Get those rubber gloves off.'

   They laugh.

Kelly I bet she farts.

Hayley I bet her fanny's on sideways.

Kelly I bet she puts it on in the mornings and then takes it off at night.

Hayley Puts it in a glass of water . . .

Diane With her husband's teeth.

Hayley And then goes . . .

Diane 'Now you may insert your penis into my

vagina . . .'

Hayley 'but take care not to fertilize my oven.'

They laugh.

Kelly (*getting carried away*) I bet she runs around with a swimming hat on, going 'Catch me if you can'.

They laugh. Diane cues Hayley to stop laughing.

Diane No, I don't fink so, Kell.

Hayley I think you got a bit carried away there, Kelly.

Diane Gone inta one.

Hayley Mad, in't she.

Kelly Since birth. I'm gonna piss meself in a minute. (*to the toilet*) Caarrm – on.

Hayley Me 'n'all (*to the toilet*) 'Urry up. You goin' toilet or building it?

Diane (*to the toilet*) You laying an egg or what?

Hayley (*to Diane and Kelly, rhetorically*) 'Ooz in there? (*to Kelly*) You goin' Typing?

Kelly Dunno. (*to Diane*) Are you?

Diane Doubt it.

Kelly So boring.

Diane You know, last time I saw Mrs Levitt I was sitting on the floor near the pipes. She comes up to me and goes, 'If you can't learn the attitude of a lady you'll never be a secretary.' I goes, 'I don't wanna be a secretary.'

Kelly What did she say?

Diane She's deaf, in't she.

Hayley In one ear. That April wants to be a journalist for magazines. She went to see her head of house about it.

Diane What did he say?

Hayley He goes that it's very competitive or something.

Diane I ain't going to see them 'bout what I want to do. They'd say I should be a slave or something.

Diane That April's a right snob.

Hayley She's got summink coming to her.

Kelly She's all right, I swear – she just don't wear the right clothes, that's all. If she'd of dressed like a swot all her life and worn National Healths, Mr Rainhill'd of given her all the info.

Diane We're all gonna get called in soon to talk about jobs.

Hayley Are we?

Diane Yeah, we gonna get interviewed.

Kelly I already had my interview. Iss borin'. I felt like they was all laughin' at me.

Diane Why?

Kelly When 'e asked me about my future, I felt like 'e was being sarcastic.

Hayley What did you say ya wanted to be?

Kelly It was on his wall. A therapist.

Diane A what rapist?

Kelly Therr-rapist.

Hayley You ain't a therapist.

Kelly Might b . . .

Diane That ain't a job, anyway. It's a hobby.

Kelly It ain't a hobby.

Hayley What is it, then?

Diane What else did he say?

Kelly Same as usual. Work hard.

Diane That all?

Kelly He said, 'I wanna see a change in you, Kelly. You've still got time. You can change.'

Diane Him? On about change? 'E don't even change his underwear, 'e don't even change his mind, let alone anything else.

Kelly My sister done all right. She ain't got her exams.

Diane They don't know what they're on about.

Hayley Oi, Diane, who are you going party with Friday night?

Diane Dunno. Might ask Paul Davies. (*beat*) Joke. Who you going with, Kell?

Kelly Dunno yet. Dunno what I'm gonna wear either.

Diane I'm wearing (*she mimes lightly as she shows Kelly*) me culottes, me . . . me wrap-over top and me . . . me black boots.

Hayley (*interrupting*) Phobia arksed me if I wanna go with him.

Kelly Who?

Hayley You know that guy, Phobia.

Diane I don't know anyone called Phobia . . .

Kelly (*seriously*) That's a girl's name, innit?

Hayley Nah, it's a state of mind.

Kelly Sounds weird.

Hayley It ain't weird.

Diane When did he ask ya – what did he say to ya?

Hayley Not that much. He kept nodding his head.

Diane How?

Hayley (*She opens her mouth and nods her head.*) Sort of like that.

Diane (*nodding her head in a slightly manic but 'cool' way*) Like this?

Hayley Yeah, and then he goes, 'All right?'

Diane (*still nodding her head*) 'All righta.' (*stopping nodding her head*) Was that it?

Diane No.

> *Diane starts to nod her head again.*

Then he puts his hands in his pockets.

Kelly Oh, I hate that.

Diane (*stopping nodding her head*) What?

Kelly Men who have a scratch . . .

Hayley He weren't scratching anything. He takes a step forward.

> *Diane takes a step forward.*

And he goes, 'You're Adam's sister, ain't ya.' I goes, 'Yeah.'

Kelly Then what did he say?

Hayley Then he goes, 'All right' again.

Diane (*nodding her head again*) 'All righta.' (*dropping her imitation*) Sounds alright.

Hayley He is all right. He's got alright hair.

Kelly What's his real name?

Hayley Dunno. Phil, I think.

Diane Phil who?

Hayley Phil Barnes.

Kelly (*suspiciously*) Weren't that who Stacey was going out with?

Hayley Yeah.

Diane You going out with Stacey's boyfriend?

Hayley I ain't 'going out with him' going out with him.

Kelly She ain't gonna be 'appy.

Hayley Well, that's her look-out.

Diane (*curious*) Is that what you really think?

Hayley Look, he asked me out.

Kelly I thought you were friends.

Hayley We were.

Diane (*morally*) You should never put a boyfriend before a mate.

Hayley Who are you to say that?

Diane All right, don't make your underwear untidy. I'm just saying . . .

Hayley (*feeling aggressive*) He's finished with Stacey.

Diane All right. I'm just saying . . . she ain't gonna be 'appy.

Kelly His brother's a right bastard, I heard.

Diane and **Hayley** Why?

Kelly Just what I heard. (*pause.*) God, I need a wee. You should of been at assembly 'smornin'. So boring.

Diane (*to Kelly*) What happened to you in Maths?

Kelly Walked out.

Diane I know, I saw that.

Hayley You walked out?

Kelly Yeah – teacher caught me looking out the window. He come up to me walkin' on the tips of his toes with his bad breath leant right over me and goes: 'Kylie, I wouldn't pay a penny for your thoughts but I would pay for a fraction of your attention.'

Diane We were doing fractions.

Hayley Yeah?

Kelly Yeah, so I goes, 'I was thinking, sir.' He started grinding up all the money in his pockets with his hands. He goes, 'You were dreaming, Kylie.' I goes, 'But what's the difference between dreaming and thinking, sir?' And he leant right over me, smellin' like a right pub lunch, I'm sure he was looking down my top . . .

Diane Didn't see anything, then.

Kelly And he goes . . . (*to Diane*) Very funny . . . (*continuing*) he goes, 'Perhaps that comment accounts for your unacademic record this term.' So I walked out.

Hayley Just like that?

Kelly I goes, 'Excuse me, sir, Nature calls' and walked out.

Hayley What did he say?

Kelly He said, 'Why are you taking a pen with you to the toilet,' so I goes, ''Cos I'm about to write something on the wall about what a fat turd you are.'

Hayley You didn't!

Kelly No, I didn't. But I could of done. (*puts on a Northern accent*) I were that mad. (*She has walked over to the mirror and looks at herself disdainfully.*) My hair. I look like a carpet. (*getting a new, fresh impetus and running back to the toilet*) 'Urry up. You fallen in there or what?

Hayley I hope you're not making a smell.

Diane Don't flush yerself away.

They bang on the door a bit then give up.

Hayley Go in that one.

Kelly No.

Hayley Go on. 'S only a Tampax.

Kelly Iss breathin', I swear.

Hayley All you got to do is flush it away.

Kelly Well, you go in there, then.

Pause.

Diane Did you kiss him?

Hayley Who?

Diane Terry or Phobia or whatever his name is.

Hayley I hardly know him.

Diane So?

Kelly So did ya?

Hayley Might of done.

Diane Tongues as well?

Hayley Oh, shut up, Diane.

Diane Did ya let him finger ya?

Hayley Yeah. And I thought I was gonna piss in his hand.

Diane Euuuuuuurgh!

Hayley Joke.

Kelly (*sighing and sinking down to the floor to sit down*) I wonder who'll be at the party.

Diane Someone tall?

Kelly With a nice bum.

Diane Soft voice.

Hayley Allright hair. (*She sits down too.*)

Kelly A car.

   Diane sits down.

Diane Warm eyes.

Kelly And warm hands.

   Pause.

Diane Last time I snogged at a party it was a nightmare.

Hayley What happened?

Diane Someone burped in my mouth.

Hayley Eurgh!

Kelly Eurgh! – what did it taste of?

Diane Cheese and onions.

Hayley Eurgh. D'ya remember your brother at that last party?

Diane Oh God. Don't bring that up.

Hayley I couldn't believe it.

Kelly What 'appened?

Hayley Ain't you 'eard this story? Diane's brother . . .

Kelly Yeah?

Hayley At Derry's party?

Kelly What?

Hayley Made a right show. He went with a girl outside in a car. Weren't even his car. Someone saw them out the window 'cos the car was rocking. Five minutes later everyone's out there watching.

Diane He's such a pig sometimes. On my life I couldn't look at him after that.

Hayley Banging on the roof, they was. Like a football match, jeering 'im on. Everyone banging on the roof. They's going – 'Tony, Tony, Tony.' I swear they thought they was in there with 'im, half o' them. Pouring beer cans on the roof, they was. Jeering, shouting. Spurting their beer. They was off their heads. Suddenly the car stops rocking. Everyone goes quiet. They start whispering 'out, out, out', then shouting 'out, out, out'. We thought they was gonna tip the car, din't we, Diane?

Diane I told you, I wen'ome.

Hayley Tony gets out of the car . . . takes a bow.

Kelly No!

Diane He was embarrassed, that's why. He's such a pig.

Hayley Girl gets out. They all started throwing things at her. I thought, God 'elp you. She had to run down the street. I saw someone pick up a stone.

Diane I'd a stoned her. What an insult. Silly cow.

Kelly Wass 'er name?

Diane She ain't from our school. She's from the convent. I think it's Jasmine summink.

Kelly My sister told me a story about her an' Phil's brother.

Hayley My Phil, Phil?

Kelly Yeah. Said he'd go with her if she put a paper bag over her head. They reckon she done it.

They react as if the story has gone too far.

Diane God.

Hayley That's low.

They fold their arms.

Kelly When was the first time you had your very first kiss?

Hayley Mine was with Marcus Wilson.

Diane Marcus Wilson?!

Kelly How old was you?

Diane It was yesterday.

Hayley 'Bout eleven. He held my hand and he goes, 'The Milky Bars are on me.' (*giggles*) I wonder what he does now?

Diane Marcus Wilson? Works up the city, I think.

Kelly How about you, Diane? How old was you when you had your first kiss with a man?

Diane About two or three.

Kelly Two or three?!

Hayley Eurgh!

Kelly Who with?

Diane A distant relative.

Hayley A distant relative?

Diane Yeah.

Kelly Who?

Diane My dad.

Kelly Oh, very clever. (*pause*) Wasser time?

Hayley Dunno.

Kelly (*to the toilet*) Hello? Are you launching a ship or what?

Hayley Why don't you go in that one?

Kelly Makes my breakfast jumpy.

Diane Iss bad luck to piss on a tampon, anyway.

Kelly Is it?

Diane Yeah. Makes you go sterile in later life.

Kelly I didn't know that. Ow'd ya know that?

Diane Written in the Bible.

Kelly What Bible?

Diane My Bible.

Kelly Nobody's ever said that . . .

Hayley I've 'eard summink like that.

Kelly It ain't true.

Diane Well, go in there, then . . .

Kelly Nah, I might catch summink off it. Did you go assembly this morning?

Hayley No, I's late.

Diane Mr White took it. He comes on, right, saying, 'I am a warrior.' I thought he meant as in carrying a spear – I had this picture of him in my head, standin' in a pair of Y-fronts. Turns out he meant 'worrier', as in stress-head.

Kelly I just thought of something.

Hayley What?

Kelly About assembly.

   Pause.

Hayley What?

Kelly Well, you know back to basics, yeah? Thirty days and all that, like they's tellin' us?

Hayley Yeah?

Kelly But I've just thought, God got Mary up the duff when she was married to someone else.

Hayley So?

Kelly So he's just like everyone else.

Hayley Men. (*pause*) I think Mr White's henpecked by his wife.

Diane He's saying something about the fact that the prime minister hasn't got very many O Levels.

Kelly That was yesterday's.

Diane Oh. Well, he was saying there's gonna be a strike on Wednesday.

Kelly We got the day off?

Hayley Excellent.

Diane We could go Southend.

Hayley London.

Diane Go Southend, on the pier.

Hayley No, go skatin'.

Kelly Yeah . . . That's out of order when they strike, innit.

Diane Yeah. Makin' free holidays for 'emselves.

Kelly We break up for summer soon, anyway.

Diane Mr White said we should do some extra reading.

Hayley Take a magazine with us.

Diane Yeah.

Kelly I had him for Social Science.

Hayley Who?

Kelly Mr White. I walked in late. He started picking on me straight away. Every excuse I come up with he said was a lie. I goes, 'This classroom reminds me of a graveyard.'

Diane You never?

Kelly I did. He wouldn't leave me alone, though, it's like he had me in his grip an' he was holding me up to the light. I had to stand there by the door. He was going, 'This class is not a graveyard, it's a breeding ground', and he was saying all what it breeds. He was going that in four or five generations' time the population from this school alone, like all our children's children's children, could make up the population of all of Essex. He goes, 'Your great-great-great-grandchildren alone, Kelly, will make up more than the population of all of us sitting in here.' He goes, 'Just think what influence the way we live our lives has on the future.' (*humouring herself*) I goes, 'Calling me a slag?'

Diane You never?

Kelly Yeah. I goes, 'School makes your hair fall out. Look at you, you're only 'bout thirty-six.'

Diane Did ya?

Kelly That's what I thought.

Hayley What did he say?

Kelly He goes, 'This is not a bald patch. It's a solar panel for a sex machine.'

Diane He's trying to be funny.

Hayley Trying to get you on his side.

Kelly I know.

Hayley My next door neighbour's pregnant. She's the same age as us.

Pause. They look uneasily at the toilet and remember what they came in for.

God, who is in there?

Kelly 'Urry up, I got urgent message.

Diane (*to the 'tampon toilet'*) Maybe thass a dead baby in there.

Hayley An alien that jumped out of someone's stomach.

Kelly An abortion . . .

Hayley That died . . .

Diane Is gonna haunt us . . .

Kelly With sounds and crying . . .

Hayley Shhhhh. I heard summink.

They stop and listen, leaning against the door of the 'tampon toilet'. It opens and they freak themselves out, screaming, etc. Diane shuts the door.

Kelly Fuckin' 'ell.

Diane (*enjoying the 'freaky atmosphere'*) 'Orrible 'bout that girl dyin'.

Kelly Yeah. Who?

Hayley In the year above.

Kelly How?

Diane Took a whole load of drugs and then passed out.

Hayley She should of just said no.

Kelly Did she die when she was still blacked out?

Hayley Yeah.

Kelly So she don't know she's dead yet.

Hayley No.

Diane She gonna die when she finds out, innit. (*to the locked toilet*) Come on, push, girl, push. I reckon she's having a baby in all (*looks in the mirror*) taking her time about it . . . God, I look a dog.

Hayley I don't know what I'd do if I got pregnant.

Diane Dog, I look a God. Oh, don't start. 'Sall my Mum goes on about. I come down with a sick bug, you should of heard her.

Kelly If I had a baby I'd 'ave to keep it in 'ere.

Diane My Mum would go mad.

Hayley Just tell her, right, that you were walking along and you slipped and fell onto an erect penis.

Kelly Naat.

Diane Only way I could persuade her I ain't gonna get a bun in the oven is if I become a nun or a lesbiand.

Kelly What did you call it?

Diane Lesbiand.

Kelly It ain't got a 'D' on the end of it.

Diane Yes it has, 'lesbiand'.

Kelly No, it hasn't, 'lesbian'.

Diane It has, Kelly: Hayley, 'as lesbian got as 'D' on the end of it?

Hayley 'D' for Danger.

Kelly 'D' for Dike.

Diane 'D' for don't do it.

Hayley Oh, come on, 'urry up in there, Slowpoke.

Kelly Are you having a slow poke or what?

Hayley God, I need a wee.

Diane Do you ever think about how lesbiands have sex?

Kelly What?

Hayley What do you mean?

Diane Well, you know. How they manage it if they haven't got all the bits.

Kelly No.

Hayley They jump up and down.

Diane Do they?

Hayley Yeah. (*demonstrating*) One puts her arms on the other's shoulders and the other one jumps.

Kelly They run at each other . . .

Diane Kelly And then bounce backwards and hit the walls.

Hayley Boing!

They laugh.

Diane That tennis player's a lesbiand.

Kelly My dad's a lesbiand.

Hayley (*calling out but not looking at the toilet*) Oyoyoyoy. What you passin', time or watah?

Kelly Does your mum ever talk to you about sex?

Hayley Yeah. Sometimes. She reckons it ain't all what it's cracked up to be. She reckons I'm lucky at my age 'cos it's all foreplay. She says sometimes that's the best bit for a woman, anyway. Don't your mum talk to you about it?

Kelly She talked to me about periods. Ages ago.

Diane My History teacher talks about periods, ages ago.

Hayley She ever tell you about her past?

Diane My History teacher talk about the past.

Kelly What like?

Hayley Like how she met your dad or whatever.

Diane That ain't history.

Kelly Nah. Only if she's 'ad a few.

Diane You can't talk about history when you're drunk. You've got to be sober for history.

Kelly (*to Diane*) What are you on about?

Diane Well, my mum reckons, right, she met my dad through this guy. His brother. She was going out with his brother first.

Hayley Really?

Kelly Weird.

Diane It gets weirder. She went out with this guy when she was about sixteen, and she reckons she went out with him 'cos he had such a lovely quiff, yeah. Then next time she saw him he was walking down the road and he was completely bald . . . not a hair on his head. She was shocked, she goes, 'What's happened to your hair.' Shining, his head was. He just ignored her.

Hayley Did he?

Diane Yeah, walked straight past her.

Hayley Then what happened?

Diane Then next time she saw him he had a full head of hair again.

Kelly What?!

Diane I know – turns out they were identical twins. One had hair, the other didn't.

Hayley You're making it up.

Diane I swear on my life. My dad's brother is his twin, and even to this day he's got a full head of hair.

Kelly Wait, what, you mean your mum went for the bald one in the end?

Diane Yeah.

Kelly Your dad ain't bald.

Diane That's a wig. I swear . . . and my brother was born five months after they was married.

Kelly Weird.

Diane That's history.

Kelly My mum reckoned she had to be in at nine.

Hayley Yeah? That's another Jackanory in 'all.

Kelly When she gets annoyed she tells me she met my dad after I was born. Says I was an artificial extermination. That's when we have rows, she don't stop.

Diane (*boldly*) My mum had to try to do an artificial thing on my brother.

Hayley A what?

Diane (*less boldly*) You know, an extermination . . .

Hayley An abortion?

Diane Sort of. She had to do it herself.

Kelly Like . . .?

Diane Like she got really drunk and she had to try and use a coat hanger and hot baths and all that.

Kelly Fuckin' 'ell.

Diane I know.

Hayley (*as if to clear up a 'messy' conversation*) Shame it didn't work.

Diane is offended.

Kelly I had a really weird dream last night.

Hayley Did ya?

Diane I hate people talking about their dreams . . .

Hayley Oh, shut up, Diane, I wanna know now.

Kelly She don't wanna know.

Diane It's borin'. Oy, Hayley. (*She points to the 'tampon toilet'.*) That ain't a tampax in there. It's a piece of your brain.

Hayley Yeah?

They lock eyes. Diane breaks it.

Diane It's your lunch.

Hayley Ya future.

Kelly It's ya boyfriend.

Hayley And mine.

Diane Who is in there?

Hayley Someone who's topped theirself.

Kelly Locked the door.

Diane Like that girl.

Kelly Had enough of the hype . . .

Diane And the tripe . . .

Kelly And the getting it right.

Pause. Diane walks off and looks round the walls. At some point when Kelly and Hayley aren't looking she writes on the wall.

Hayley D'you row a lot wiv your mum?

Kelly She's worried I'm gonna go like my sister. But I ain't.

Hayley What does she say?

Kelly (*doing a parody*) 'You wanna watch out, you wanna look after yourself in this world. Ain't no one else gonna.'

Then if ever she's had a bit too much she goes (*over-emotional voice*) 'I love you, you know I love ya, don't ya. You know it, don't ya, I love you darlin'.' She reckons I should give up school, but I dunno.

Hayley Your sister doin' all right?

Kelly Yeah.

Hayley She still moved out?

Kelly Yeah.

Hayley How often do you see her?

Kelly Sometimes.

Hayley Do you see her baby?

Kelly Yeah. Why?

Hayley Just wonderin'. Aunty Kelly.

Diane Aunty Kelly.

Kelly (*defensive*) Can't talk yet.

Diane Oy, Hayley, there's something written about you on the wall here.

Hayley What. (*reads*) 'Hayley is a bitch.' Bloody bitches, who wrote that?

Diane Someone's got it in for ya.

Hayley Who the fuck wrote that?

Kelly I wonder who?

Hayley I'll find out.

Kelly D'ya reckon it might be Stacey?

Hayley Bloody bitches.

Diane Weren't in here yesterday.

Hayley Wait till I see her.

Diane Why, what you gonna say to her?

Hayley What am I gonna do to her, more like.

Kelly You gonna pick a fight with her?

Diane She's quite hard, Hayley.

Kelly You don't know it was her.

Hayley It's bound to have been her. Who else would it of been?

Kelly and Diane look at each other.

Going around dirtying my name.

Kelly What are you gonna say to her?

Hayley I'll just walk up to her and I'll go – 'Oi, Stacey . . .'

Diane Yeah?

Hayley I'll go – 'Oi, Stacey . . .'

Diane Pardon me, but . . .

Hayley No, I'll go, 'What's my name,' and then I'll go, 'My name is bird.' (*pauses to think*) Then I'll go, 'Yes, you heard, it's bird or turd or nerd,' then I'll just reel off all these names.

Diane Like?

Hayley Boring cow, silly cow . . .

Kelly Don't know how . . .

Diane Eejit . . .

Hayley Needs it . . .

Diane Desper-it . . .

Kelly Harl-it . . .

Diane Old witch . . .

Hayley Skanky bitch . . .

Kelly Lanky bitch . . .

Diane Cranky bitch . . .

Hayley I'll go to her, 'You should of heard the vicar at my christening, he blushed. Slow poke, bad joke.

Diane Time of the week . . .

Kelly Bit of a geek . . .

Hayley You should see my passport. It's like a book. Misled Stresshead . . .

Diane Underfed, overfed . . .

Kelly Under-read . . .

Hayley Dud . . .

Kelly Stud . . .

Diane No, I ain't never been called a stud.

Kelly Hoara . . .

Hayley Flora . . .

Diane Goofy . . .

Kelly Aloofy . . .

Hayley Frumpy . . .

Kelly Dumpy . . .

Hayley Lumpy . . .

Kelly Grumpy . . .

Diane Dog brain . . .

Kelly Dog breath . . .

Hayley Death . . .

Kelly Bit of stuff . . .

Hayley Up the duff . . .

Diane Yeees please, Cock tease . . .

Hayley Shut up . . .

Kelly Stuck up . . .

Diane Fucked up . . .

Hayley Me. And then I'll go . . . 'Despite this wealth of names, my mother calls me Hayley.'

Kelly That should shut her up.

Diane She'll probly come up to you and go: crack.

Diane goes to do a mock slap around Hayley's face, but Hayley catches her hand. They look in each other's eyes fiercely for a second – then, as if to relieve the tension . . .

Hayley Do what?

Diane (*calmly*) Let go.

Hayley Then I'll go like this . . .

Hayley, still holding Diane's hand, punches her on the arm.

Diane (*retreating*) Ow, you bitch, that hurt.

Hayley (*carelessly*) Sorry.

Diane God, you're as bad as my . . .

Hayley Sorry, it weren't that hard.

Diane She'll probly come up behind you like this. (*She* *grabs Hayley's hair*.)

Hayley Yeah, then I'll do this. (*She tries to get at Diane but Diane keeps a hold on her hair.*)

Kelly Leave it out, both of ya. Let go, Diane. Anyone coulda wrote that.

Hayley Calling me a bitch?

Diane (*still pulling at Hayley's hair*) How you feeling, Hayley?

Hayley Get off me.

Diane She'd of had you by now, wouldn't she?

Hayley (*struggling*) Get off.

Diane 'Cos she'd of gone like this (*tugs Hayley's hair*).

Hayley Oooooooow! (*She twists free.*) God, what did ya do that for, you stupid bitch?

Diane Sorry.

> *Hayley walks away from her, rubbing her head and looking around the walls.*

Hayley (*pointing to the opposite half of the room*) You'd better keep to that half of the toilet.

Diane I will.

Kelly You two are mad.

Diane (*playing with the words*) What goes around comes around.

Hayley You're mad, Diane.

Diane Yeah, I know, since birth.

Hayley This weren't even your fight.

Diane Might of been.

Hayley What do you think I am, a free-for-all?

Diane No. (*almost sarcastic but with emphasis*) Sorry, Hayley, sorry. (*patronizing*) Look, I'm drawing a line down the middle, all right? (*drawing the line with her finger*) Down the middle.

Hayley (*sarcastically, under her breath, laughing*) Yeah.

Diane (*finishing her line*) There we go.

Hayley Fuck off, Diane.

Diane (*still taking the piss*) Oooh!

Kelly (*to the toilet*) Come on, you fat cow, you drowned or what? Wasser time?

Hayley I don't reckon anyone's in there.

Kelly Course there's someone in there – it's locked. (*sighs*) Wasser time?

Hayley Someone's topped theirself.

Diane Had enough of the hype.

Hayley And the tripe.

Kelly And the gettin' it right.

Hayley They flush theirself away.

Diane They're history now.

Hayley They're biology.

Kelly They're geography.

Hayley I don't reckon anyone's in there.

Kelly Course there's someone in there. It's locked. (*sighs*) Wasser time?

Hayley Maybe we should go down the high street.

Diane I look like a doormat today. I feel like a carpet. You didn't 'alf hurt my arm.

Kelly How do you know Stacey ain't going out with Phobia to the party?

Hayley 'Cos I asked him, 'What about Stacey?' and he goes, 'I ditched her.'

Diane God, this place is an arsehole.

Kelly Wasser time?

Hayley You going History?

Kelly Dunno. Are you, Diane?

Diane Dunno.

Hayley (*knocking on the toilet door more violently with her fist and shouting*) Come on!

Kelly (*joining in thumping*) Fucking 'urry up.

Diane walks away, oblivious to them.

Diane (*looking in the mirror*) I'm going party, though.

BLACKOUT

Act Two: The Holiday

The second floor of a council flat in Tilbury. **Kim** *sits at the kitchen table, her head resting on her arms. She is bent double and could be asleep. A nappy sticks out of the top of the bin. Baby's utensils, like a rattle or bottle, are mixed with a general debris of dirty cups, a packet of false nails or nail varnish, a hair brush, a plate with crumbs on, etc. A tinny radio is tuned to Kiss FM. A baby intercom is near Kim. Backstage is a window and curtains.*

Kim is in her nightie, with her dressing gown draped over her shoulders as she rests.

The buzzer from the door bell is heard. Then a banging is heard on the door below. Kim barely moves. the banging continues and gets louder.

*Kim 'comes to'. She sits up quite still and listens. The voice of a young woman (**Karen**) is heard calling from the street below.*

Karen Kim, Ki-im. (*pause*) Kim.

Kim is relieved. She begins to look for her keys.

Kim.

Kim walks to the window. She opens the curtains, then the window.

Kim What?

Karen It's me.

Kim Oh's you. 'Ang on. (*She walks to the table and finds her keys under something. She walks to the window.*) Eeyar. Catch. (*She throws the keys out of the window.*)

Karen Oops. (*She has dropped them.*)

Kim closes the curtains. She turns off the radio, twists her hair up. She looks a bit indecisive, then sits down at the kitchen table again and lights a cigarette. Enter Karen.

Oi, Kim, there's a massive turd outside your door.

Kim What?

Karen Pwor, dark in 'ere, innit. Smells, innit? You been asleep? Iss beautiful outside, Kim. Yesterday is raining. Today is like Spain. I been up the market. Bought a pair of shoes. What ja fink, Kim? Only 12.99. Nearly ruined 'em. Only missed it by a quarter of an inch.

Kim I thought you was Mark.

Karen I put 'em on soon as I got 'em. Stood there in the 'igh street in me bare feet like a bleedin' 'ippy. Iss the sort of day for it, though. Them stairs is like Mount 'ave-a-rest. Given me 'eadache. Given me sweaty buttocks 'n' all. Smells in 'ere. Mus' be the dark. I'm gonna 'ave to take me shoes off. Smell even more then. Was you dreamin'? Shall I open the window? You all right? You 'ad vandals in 'ere or what? (*pause*) You thought I was who?

Kim Mark.

Karen Oh. What ja fink the time is?

Kim Dunno. 'Bout eleven.

Karen Iss one.

Kim Oh. Time flies, innit.

Karen There's a bloke opposite painting his house. (*She makes a 'wanker sign'*).

Kim Oh.

Karen Mark been up 'ere?

Kim Yeah.

Karen Wass 'e want?

Kim Dunno. Dunno if 'e knows.

Karen Kim, iss beautiful outside. I got a free tour of it 'cos the friggin' bus driver wouldn't let me on the bus. I 'ad to walk all the way up 'ere nearly, 'sept Shell gave me a lift when I got right to the top of the 'ill. I's short of the bus fare. Bleedin' wanker wouldn't let me on. I goes, 'I could be raped.' 'E goes, 'It's broad daylight.' I said, 'Din't you 'ear about that bus driver 'oo got bottled. That was broad daylight.' 'E said, 'You threatnin' me?' I said, 'I's statin' a fact.' 'E said, 'If you was my daughter I'd kick you up the arse.' I said, 'If you was my father I wouldn't feel it.' I said, 'If you was my father I wouldn't 'ave an arse. I'd be deformed. If you was my father I'd be 'omeless,' I said, 'If you was my father me and me mum'd of been long gone so ya needn't bleedin' worry.' Bleedin' jaffa. Stupid prick. If I'd of seen 'im up the pub e'd be buyin' me a drink. Bet 'e don't go up the pub. Bet 'e sits at 'ome wiv 'is wife eatin' 'is children. What ja fink, Kim? Dark in 'ere. What ya been doin'? Sittin' in?

Kim Yeah.

Karen (*taking a cigarette from a pack on the table*) Wanna fag?

Kim They're mine, anyway, in't they.

Karen Can I 'ave one?

Kim You got one.

Karen I know. (*pause*) You got a light, Kim?

Kim chucks her the lighter.

Ta. (*She lights it and takes a puff as though enjoying it.*) I 'ate B&H. B&H is for cunts, innit. Used to say that. D'ya remember? 'B&H is for cunts.' 'Ere, I seen your sister walkin' up the road, Kim. She grown, in't she? Nearly. She supposed to be in school, in't she. Bunkin' off, I bet, little mare. Less open up the curtains. I's like a morgue in 'ere wivout the dead people. I's walkin' up. All sun shinin'. My 'eels was sinkin' inta the pavement like mud, I's so 'ot.

Kim Leave the winda, Kal.

Karen Is it?

Kim Yeah.

Karen (*accusingly*) There's a poo outside your door.

Kim Is there?

Karen Yeah. Wonder 'oo done it. Weren't you, was it, Kim? (*Slight pause*) I din't tell ya about Michelle's car, did I? Iss excellent, iss red. She got megabass, everything. We's goin' along. She picked me up. BOOMchikkaBOOM chikkaBOOMchikkaBOOM. Is excellent. Iss red. 'Ow long since you seen your sister?

Karen Not long.

Karen Grown a bit in't she, nearly.

Kim Yeah.

Karen We could go outside later. I didn't tell Michelle I liked 'er car. She'd take it for a compliment for 'er not 'er car. She don't know what she wants less everyone else wants it 'n' all. She's mad like that. And 'er mum. They're a right pair of fannies. 'Er mum always looks like someone's surprised 'er from behind, innit. She's so tight when she farts it squeaks, I bet. Shell's so tight when she farts it squeaks so high only dogs can hear it, no one else. I arksed 'er if she give me drivin' lessons. She said I ain't insured. Thass an excuse, innit. Where's Daniel? 'E asleep?

Kim Yeah.

Karen Ya been out, Kim? Iss pretty 'ot. Well iss more than pretty 'ot. Iss fuckin' 'ot. People goin' topless out there. Men, anyway. You can 'ave a look in my bags if ya wanna, Kim. I been down the market. They got all sorts down there, dirt cheap. I seen Vera, me mum's sister's mate. I fought, blimey, ain't seen 'er in donkey's years. I got a pair of earrings. They got fruit, curtains, everything. Vera still come up there for her bargains. Ain't seen 'er since I's about fifteen. Two years, innit. Funny jus' bump into 'er. 'Er daughter's moved away. Is really posh where she's gone. Ya walk round there all ya smell is red cars an' chlorine. I thought lovely. Vera's lovely. Fightin' everyone up there for 'er bargains, she was. And 'avin' a laugh wiv 'em 'n' all. You all right, Kim? You slept on your 'air funny.

Kim (*self-conscious*) 'Ave I?

Karen Yeah. Ya look like a punk on one side and an 'ippy on the other. You been sleepin', innit. Dreamin'. (*pause*) D'ya know what the time is?

Kim Iss one.

Karen Iss one. (*pause*) I's readin' you're gonna 'ave refugees movin' down your street, Kim. They'll be knockin' on your door soon, 'n' all. (*slight pause*) 'S that why ya din't answer the door? (*She goes to the window and peers under the blind.*) That bloke's still paintin' 'is 'ouse. 'E's up a ladder. Go on, fall. (*She makes a game with the curtains.*) Fall. Fall. (*She gives up the game and faces Kim again. Slight pause*) I do it for ya, your 'air, if ya want. I could do it. Would ya like me to do it, Kim?

Kim Nah.

Karen Why not?

Kim You never finished your trainin', did ya.

Karen I done all the cuttin'. Is jus all the words an that I don't know.

Kim How much?

Karen What?

Kim How much ?

Karen (*genuinely pissed off*) Oh, come off it, Kim.

There is silence for a while.

Daniel sick? Ain't he sleepin'? I wen' up the job centre, Kim. I tell ya what, I'd be sorted if I's a welder. So 'oo else been up 'ere? Anyone been up 'ere, Kim. Any phone calls? Pwor, it's 'ot. Does it depress ya, smokin' the wrong brand of cigarettes, Kim? Depresses me. We could go outside later.

Karen finds another 'game' with an object near her or something, then she gets bored with it and moves on to the following game. Pause.

Pwor, dear. Huf. (*Karen crosses her legs, looks at Kim.*) Huf. (*She uncrosses her legs, looks at Kim.*) Huf. (*She crosses her legs again, looks at Kim.*)

Kim What ya doin'?

Karen Tha's what fat people do when they cross their legs, they go 'huf'.

Kim No, they don't.

Karen Yes, they do.

Kim Calling me fat?

Karen Yeah. And paranoid.

222

Pause. Kim resolves the tension by referring to an old 'routine' they used to have.

Kim I got a right to be paranoid. I got a right to be what I want.

Karen I am not just a number.

Kim I am a free man.

Karen Woo-man.

Kim Womb-man.

They laugh a bit.

So what ya comin' round for?

Karen Jus ta see ya.

Kim You been doin' much?

Karen I'm tryin' to save up, in I.

Kim Oh, what, might ya still be goin' away?

Karen Yeah.

Kim Bought much for it?

Karen What, me 'oliday?

Kim Yeah.

Karen Not yet. Dunno if I can go yet. Saw Sarah the other night, though.

Kim Did ya?

Karen Yeah, she was out having a right rave. Dancing about. Iss 'er last night 'fore they put her on nights.

Kim Fought she said she ain't never gonna do nights.

Karen I know. She's going mad for the 'oliday. She wants all the clothes, spendin' money, everything. She goin' mad for it.

Kim She gonna go wevver you go or not?

Karen Yeah.

Kim Wants to get away?

Karen Yeah.

Kim 'Cos of 'er dad?

Karen Yeah. 'Ere, Kim, I din't tell ya about the funeral, did I? Sarah tell ya about it?

Kim Ain't seen 'er.

Karen 'Parently it was a right weird day 'cos she ain't seen 'er dad in years, 'as she?

Kim I'm surprised Sarah's mum went.

Karen I think she only went to give Sarah a bit of support. Or tha's what she said, anyway. But apparently she ended up embarrassing Sarah a bit. Right in the middle of the funeral she stood up.

Kim Did she?

Karen Yeah. Right in the middle of the vicar's speech, she stood up. Vicar was goin' on about what a great man Sarah's dad had been. Payin' his respec's to him in a speech. Sarah's mum stood up (*she stands up*) and went 'Sorry' jus' like that in the middle.

Kim Out of the blue?

Karen Out of the blue like that. Then she walked up to the coffin an went 'Sorry' again, like that. Everyone thought she was apologizing to 'im for all the rows they'd 'ad, even though 'e's dead. They was really touched.

Kim Ah.

Karen But Sarah's mum reckons, she told me later, that she jus' got this feelin' that she's at the wrong funeral. She stood up to go. Then she wen' over to the coffin to check iss 'im in there. And when she saw it was she realize she made a mistake.

Kim Made a mistake?

Karen Yeah. She was in the right place. Sarah 'ad to 'old 'er mum up 'stead of the other way round. When they put 'er dad inta the ground, 'er mum made this noise (*she makes an involuntary gasping sound*) like that. 'Orrible realizin' you're in the wrong place, innit.

Kim presses the intercom. Loud sound of a baby crying.

Wassat? Intercom?

Kim Yeah.

Karen 'S weird, innit. (*pause*) Ya gonna go inta 'im?

Kim In a minute.

Karen 'Ere, Kim, sorry I din't come back 'ere the other night.

Kim 'S all right.

Karen I went back to Lee's.

Kim Blimey. You're going it a bit, intcha?

Karen (*girlishly*) You annoyed?

Kim (*lightly*) Nah. Do what ya want.

Karen (*womanly*) I don't care any more. Since I left Darren I ain't giving a shit.

Kim You're gonna 'urt yourself.

Karen Nah. I'm indestructible now. Life's an adventure, innit. To be lived. Iss funny not livin' wiv someone. I only lived wiv Darren 'cos I didn't wanna live at 'ome. Actually tha's not true. But ja know what I mean?

Kim Yeah.

Karen Ya live with them so ya know what iss gonna be like when ya marry 'em. Then ya don't wanna marry 'em no more. Ja know what I mean?

Kim I ain't ever lived with a man, 'ave I?

Karen I reckon marriage is going out.

Kim Why?

Karen I don't wanna make the same mistakes as me mum, do you? Hangin's gone out. They don't drown no one no more. I reckon marriage is goin' out 'n' all. Ya reckon Mark'll be back, then?

Kim Dunno. (*slight pause*) So wass this bloke like, then?

Karen 'E's lovely. When 'e blows in my ear I feel like it comes out somewhere else.

Kim D'ya really like 'im?

Karen Yeah.

Kim D'ya think you could love 'im?

Karen I dunno. Dunno what love is no more. Dunno if I care either. What about you, Kim?

Kim What?

Karen (*ignoring the fact Kim won't join in*) And love. Is jus' when 'e kisses me, I sort of feel . . . I sort of feel like I've been Tangoed. 'E is good with 'is 'ands. Most men think 'cos they know where it is they've found it. 'E ain't like that. 'E's got a touch.

Kim Wass 'e do?

Karen 'E's a butcher.

Kim Eurrgh!

Karen What?

Kim All that raw meat.

Karen Oh, stop it. You're gonna put me off, 'n' all. (*pause*) You met anyone, Kim?

Kim What?

Karen Met anyone?

Kim What, like you do?

Karen Yeah, like me.

Kim I don't feel very turned on lately.

Karen You 'avin' a menopause?

Kim Dunno. I did meet one bloke.

Karen Yeah.

Kim Taxi driver.

Karen Yeah? Wass 'e like? I might know 'im.

Kim Ya don't know 'im.

Karen I might. Bit of all right, is 'e?

Kim 'E's quite nice.

Karen Quite lively, is he?

Kim 'E's all right.

Karen When ya seein' 'im?

Kim Dunno. 'E's got a girlfriend. I ain't seein' 'im.

Karen Ya never know ya luck, she might be ugly.

Kim She's pregnant.

Karen What? Oh, forget it.

Kim I know.

Karen 'Ow d'ya know she's pregnant?

Kim 'E told me.

Karen What. 'E's chattin' you up an 'e goes, 'Oh and by the way my girlfriend's pregnant'?

Kim It weren't like that, 'e weren't chattin' me up.

Karen Oh, don't tell me you're just friends, I 'ate all that rubbish.

Kim No, you ain't gettin' it. We's just talkin'. 'E said 'e feels freer with me than with 'is girlfriend.

Karen Free? You don't wanna make someone feel free, Kim. Ya wanna make 'em feel attached.

Kim What, like you?

Karen Yeah, like me.

Kim Oh, I dunno why I'm boverin'.

Karen Oh cheers. So 'ow did 'e leave it wiv ya?

Kim 'E's gonna ring me.

Karen Does 'e know about Daniel?

Kim Yeah, 'e don't mind.

Karen I should think not, rate 'e's goin'.

Kim Karen, you ain't listenin'.

Karen I am. I don't like the sound of 'im. 'E sounds V.D.

Kim Wassat?

Karen Very dodgy.

Kim You ain't even met him.

Karen I don't 'ave to. I can tell. Has 'e got C.F.?

Kim Wassat?

Karen Cash flow.

Kim Dunno.

Karen 'E's gonna need one. Steer clear of 'im. Sounds like a sex maniac. 'E could be anyone.

Kim What ya bein' so down on 'im for?

Karen Don't like the sound of 'im. All that freedom. What is he? A feminist?

Kim Oh, but iss all right for you to be goin' round wiv different and older men?

Karen That ain't the same.

Kim Why?

Karen 'Cos ya should be careful.

Kim Why?

Karen I 'ope 'e's good lookin' for all this hassle.

Kim 'E's all right. I ain't that interested, anyway. I shouldn'a told ya.

Karen I'd still like to meet 'im. What about Mark, though?

Kim Don't ask me. Can't stand 'im. Bloody pisshead.

Karen 'E been tryin' a get back wiv ya, innit.

Kim Don't know what 'e wants. Don't fink 'e knows. 'E been out there about half an hour this mornin', standin'

outside the winda shoutin' ''E's my blood, 'e's my blood.'
Fuckin' 'bout half hour. I din't let 'im in. Din't even go to
the winda. 'E'll be back.

Karen Blimey. Should a call the police.

Kim (*like it's a bad idea*) Yeah.

Karen Did ya jus' stay in 'ere?

Kim Yeah. Wen' asleep.

Karen Ya wen' asleep?

Kim I sat waitin' for 'im to go. Then I got up. Fed Daniel
'cos 'e's cryin'. Put him sleep. Put me music on. Sat 'ere
cursin' 'im. Then, tha's right, me mum phoned in a strop,
spoke to 'er, then I must of dropped off meself, 'cos I 'ad a
right weird dream an' I slep' on me 'air funny.

Karen Blimey. D'ya think 'e'll be back?

Kim Dunno.

  Pause.

Karen (*giving up*) 'Ow's ya mum, 'ow comes she's in a
strop, then?

Kim She's all right. We 'ad a row, tha's all.

Karen What about?

Kim Social. Social worker wen' round 'er 'ouse. Me mum
reckons I sent 'er roun' there.

Karen You've got a social worker?

Kim Yeah.

Karen 'Ow comes?

Kim I din't ask for one, it just happened.

Karen Wass she like?

Kim Bit uptight. All right. She wears long skirts.

Karen Oh blimey. She skinny or fat?

Kim Dunno. Bit of both.

Karen She any good at 'er job?

Kim Sort of, yeah.

Karen She ask ya lots of questions?

Kim Yeah. First time I met her she asked me if I 'ad any 'obbies. I thought, fuck off.'

Karen Yeah, fuck off. What she ask ya that for?

Kim Dunno.

Karen I bet ya din't ask her what her hobbies are. I bet she's got too many of 'em, whatever they are.

Kim Nah, she's all right.

Karen Ain't she got nothin' better to do than hobbies?

Kim Dunno.

Karen Does she smell of incense sticks? So 'ow's Daniel? Fink 'e's gone asleep?

Kim Dunno.

Karen 'E been askin' after me?

Kim 'E can't talk yet.

Karen I know. Was a joke. 'Ere, I've got an 'obbie, Kim. Swimmin'. D'ya fancy goin' swimmin'?

Kim Not really.

Karen Go on, we can take Daniel wiv us.

Kim What, an' drown 'im?

Karen Poor little sod.

Kim 'E is a little sod, an' all. 'E 'ad me up all night last night nearly.

Karen So did my bloke. Was 'e sick?

Kim Yeah.

Karen So was my bloke.

Kim presses the baby intercom. Sound of a baby crying.

Workin' 'imself into a state, inne.

Kim I go inta 'im. Whajja wanna go swimmin' for, anyway?

Karen You should see me in my bikini.

Kim Ya don't wanna lose weight?

Karen Na I wanna put some on. I look like a stick. If I was to lay on a beach long enough, someone'd come an' pick me up an' throw me for their dog. I wanna build up me muscles. I can't eat unless I'm 'ungry. Swimmin' makes me 'ungry.

Kim I wish I 'ad that problem.

Karen Least ya got chests. I ain't got chests.

Kim Ya wanna 'ave a baby if ya want chests.

Karen I don't want a baby.

Pause. They go off into their own worlds.

Do you fancy goin' away, Kim? Where would you wanna go if we was to go away? Seychelles? Malibu? Could go away somewhere. Lie on a golden beach somewhere.

Kim smiles. They know this dream.

Sip Malibu in the Seychelles. Pick up seashells in Malibu.

Pick up a couple of Spanish geezers. Or whatever sort of geezers they 'ave there. Boogie all night. Sleep it off on the beach. (*sings*) Ain't no stoppin' us now, we're on the move.

Kim (*backing her*) Ooh. Ooh. Ooh.

Karen Ain't no stoppin' us now . . .

Kim and Karen We're on the groove . . . (*They dance a bit.*)

Kim Ooh. Ooh. Ooh.

Karen Ooh. Ooh. Ooh . . . The night was growin' old but she had saved one last dance for the dawn. Whaddya reckon, Kim? Could go away. Like Sarah. Start savin' up, innit. (*pause*) We could go up the park later. Ain't chargin' us for air yet, innit.

Kim I once seen me social worker up the park.

Karen (*a bit suspicious*) What doin'?

Kim She weren't workin'. I think she was wiv 'er mates. This bloke an' a woman. They looked like a couple, an' there was 'er. She din't look like a gooseberry, though. She look like she was really enjoyin' 'erself. She looked totally different.

Karen Everyone looks different outside of work, innit.

Kim Yeah. 'S funny. I watched 'er for ages. She din't see me. I was wiv Daniel. 'E's in 'is pram. An' when she went to say goodbye to 'em both she kissed 'em both on both cheeks. Nice, innit. I jus' walked on.

Karen Is she French?

Kim Tha's what me mum said. 'Er and the social worker 'ad a row the other day.

Karen Did they?

Kim Me mum shut the door in 'er face.

Karen Blimey.

Kim Yeah, I know when she went 'cos me mum phoned me that night. Is the other Thursday, it was.

Karen So what 'appened?

Kim Well, 'parently me mum 'ad 'ad a leaving party at work – they'd all gone up the pub that lunchtime so she was a bit off 'er nut – come home to 'ave a lie down, there's a knock at the door an' it's this social woman. She goes, 'Are you Mrs Gibson?' Me mum goes, 'What's it to you?' She goes, 'Are you the grandmother of Daniel Gibson?' or summink. Anyway. That gets right up me mum's nose. She goes, 'Don't you call me a granny.' She goes, 'I'm thirty-seven and not a day older. Thirty-seven to the day, I am.'

Karen What did social say?

Kim Dunno. She should of said 'Appy Birthday, but she goes summink about that she has to follow a procedure or summink. All I know is that me mum nearly 'ad a cow when she said 'ad she been drinkin', and she goes summink about the procedure again to her an' my mum goes, 'Go an' get a boyfriend. Get a bit of colour in ya cheeks and then come back and stand on me doorstep an' we'll see if ya still got a face like a slapped arse.' So Melony, or whatever her name is, is on about me mum drinking now.

Karen She is sticking her nose in, in't she? What ya gonna do?

Kim Dunno. I said to her, 'Look, I don't want you coming round 'ere calling my family names.' She goes that she's tryin' to 'elp. I said, 'Help?' I said, 'You're makin' it so I won't be able to go out no more if you're on about me mum.' I said, 'I only leave 'im wiv 'er now an' then 'cos she works an' she's got her own life,' I said, 'but I won't even be able to do that now.'

Karen Where's your mum workin' now?

Kim She got a couple of jobs.

Karen I want a proper job. I'm sick of all this cash in 'and. Don't get ya nowhere. I want a little nest egg. Couple of fiva-livas to keep each other company. Don't wanna work up the Nags no more.

Kim Wish she 'adn't gone up me mum's.

Karen Bloody social. Wass she like to you?

Kim Me? She's all right. She might be sorting me out some babysitting like, official. I s'pose I feel two ways about it.

Karen 'Ow comes you've got a social worker, though? What, ja jus get one when you 'ave a baby?

Kim 'Cos of all me fines an' that.

Karen What fines ya got?

Kim TV licence. Shopliftin' fine . . .

Karen I could lend ya some money, Kim.

Kim You owe me some money.

Karen Do I?

Kim Nah's only a joke.

Karen What did ja nick?

Kim What did I nick? (*She feels a bit defensive but then realizes she doesn't care.*) Packet of jelly tots. An' a can of beans. Weight Watchers.

Karen Weight Watchers?

They laugh.

Where'd ya hide it?

Kim Up me sleeves.

They laugh.

I din't care. Iss jus' when I picked up Daniel (*she suddenly feels painful and she closes her eyes*) an' I went, 'Fuckin' 'ell.'

Pause.

Karen You sure I don't owe you no money, Kim?

Kim Karen, issa joke.

Karen So 'ow much do I owe ya?

Kim Ya don't owe me nothin'.

Karen Suit yaself.

Kim Don't get an arse-ache about it.

Karen I ain't. If I owe ya summink I wanna give it ya. Summink's new in 'ere. Wass new in 'ere?

Kim Baby bath.

Karen Where?

Kim Over there.

Karen Where ja get that?

Kim Christenin'.

Karen Thought it was a UFO. You could sell stuff from the christenin', you ever thought of that, Kim? That chain cost me a bit, I can tell ya. 'Ere, Kim, I do owe you a fiver, don' I?

Kim Do ya?

Karen I jus' remembered, that taxi, weren't it?

Kim Oh, yeah. Oh, well.

Karen Oh, Kim.

Kim That was ages ago.

Karen I got it 'ere. (*She fishes a fiver out of her pocket.*)

Kim Don't want it.

Karen Take it.

Kim No.

  Pause.

Karen Shake my hand, Kim.

Kim Nah.

Karen Shake my hand.

  *Kim shakes Karen's hand. When Kim pulls her hand
  away there is a fiver in it. Kim puts it on the table.*

Right. I'm chuckin' it on the floor.

  *She throws it on the floor. They watch where it lands.
  They look at it.*

Kim I don't want it.

Karen Take it.

Kim What is it? Rubbish?

Karen It ain't rubbish, it's got a geezer with a wig on it
and everything.

Kim That's the Queen. (*pause*) I got a phone call from the
social. Reckon they're cuttin' off me money.

Karen Why?

Kim 'Cos me book's gone missing.

Karen They can't stop your money 'cos of your book.

Kim They reckon I sold it, 'cos someone else has been drawing out off of it.

Karen Do what?

Kim Signing on in my name.

Karen They reckon you sold it?

Kim Yeah, they can do me for it as well.

Karen (*confidential*) Did ya sell it?

Kim No.

Karen Bastards. 'Ere, this woman at the bus stop asked me to put me cigarette out. Was me last one. Said she don't wanna be a passive smoker. I said to 'er, 'Mind your own business.' I said, 'You're gonna get cancer anyway. All the diesel. All the worry 'bout passive smokin'.' I says, 'You're gonna get it, anyway.' She nearly kicked the shit outta me. She talk so much I thought her boobs was gonna drop off. An' mine. Maybe they 'ave. No, still there. Hard to tell, innit. Fwor, dear. Huf.

Kim Oh, stop doin' that.

Karen Pick up that money, will ya, Kim. Otherwise Daniel'll eat it or summink.

Kim Iss yours?

Karen Iss yours. A debt's a debt. Is Mark looking for work?

Kim Doubt it.

Karen Iss hot outside, Kim.

Kim Is it? How hot is it?

Karen All the dogs in the neighbourhood are lying down. Oh, pick up that fiver, will ya?

Kim Where is it?

Karen You're gonna be annoyed at yourself if you hoover it up. D'ya fink Daniel's all right? Did 'e 'ave ya up all night?

Kim Yeah. I jus' about got 'im off to sleep an' then bloody Mark come round.

Karen Yah gonna go inta him?

Kim Yeah. I'll go inta him. (*She gets up and picks up the five pound note.*) Wonder 'oo 'ad this last.

Karen Me.

Kim Before you. Goes through lots of 'ands, money, don't it?

Karen (*slight parody of an Essex girl*) Queen's been through more pairsa hands than I have.

Kim Eeyar, Kal. I'll put it on 'ere case either of us needs it.

Karen You should get a court order out on Mark. Or the police.

Kim What, 999?

Karen Yeah.

Kim I'm gonna go inta Daniel. Where's 'is bottle?

Karen Yah bottle feedin' 'im?

Kim Yeah. 'E bites.

Karen Does he? Ow.

Kim Yeah. 'E's bitten me. 'E can be right spiteful sometimes. So I'm stickin' 'im on a bottle.

Karen So 'e ain't gonna get all the breast no more. Poor little sod. Oh, well, that'll teach 'im. 'Don't bite the boob that feeds ya.' Ya gonna feed 'im, then? S'pose I better go.

Kim looks uncomfortably at Karen. She doesn't want her to go yet.

Kim D'ya wanna cup of tea?

Karen Wouldn't mind.

Kim See if ya can find 'is bottle while you're up, will ya.

Karen Oy, ya bitch. Is it nice breast feedin', Kim?

Kim You ain't finkin' of 'avin' a baby, are ya?

Karen (*wistfully*) Dunno.

Kim (*importantly*) Iss a big decision.

Karen I know. Wass it like bein' pregnant?

Kim 'Sall right.

Karen Just 'all right'?

Kim Nah, iss more than all right. I quite miss it. Iss not like when ya grow ya boobs or whatever, iss different. Iss jus' inside. Like a secret.

Karen D'ya wish ya could pop 'im back up there?

Kim When 'e bawls at me I bawl at 'im back. 'E goes 'Waaa', I go 'Waaa'.

Karen presses the intercom. Sound of baby crying.

Karen Waaaaa, Daniel.

Kim Waaaaa.

Karen lets the intercom go.

Karen 'E's got a mood on today, in 'e. Less take 'im up the park.

Kim An' leave 'im there. Don't wanna go out of 'ere 'cos of Mark.

Karen Why dun't yah call the police?

Kim Nah. I ain't calling them. They'll arrest me, 'n' all.

Karen You told the social?

Kim Yeah, she reckons I can get a court order out on 'im. She don't know, though. All 'is family live round 'ere.

Karen Ya told ya mum?

Kim Ya know what she used to be like. Giving 'im coffee, 'How are you, Mark', all that. Well in there, he used to be, and he knew it. (*pause*) He wen' up 'er 'ouse the other day.

Karen She din't let 'im in?

Kim Nah, not now.

Karen Blimey.

Kim One minute she's one way an' the next minute she's the other, innit.

Karen She just wanted you two . . .

Karen and **Kim** . . . To get back together.

Kim I know. (*flicks her cigarette*) Why can't everyone mind their own. 'Sall I hear now. The baby, the baby, the baby.

Karen Fink ya might try that bloke, Kim?

Kim What, taxi driver?

Karen Yeah.

Kim Fought ya didn't fink I should.

Karen Don't mean ya shouldn't.

Kim Ain't got the money to keep goin' out.

Karen 'E might pay.

Kim S'pose. (*pause*) I got a whackin' great TV licence fine. Tha's from months ago. I got letters sayin' if I don't pay up they're gonna come an' arrest me.

Karen Wass the TV one?

Kim Two hundred an' twenty quid. I told ya. Two twenty quid. If I 'ad two twenty quid I wouldn't pissin' give it to them, I pissin' well go abroad if I 'ad two 'undred an' twenty quid. I feel like pissin' goin' abroad anyway. (*She sighs.*) I dunno.

Karen I'll give ya the money, Kim.

Kim (*cynically*) Will ya?

Kim picks up her cigarette packet. While Karen is talking she is lost in her own world, and just stares at the packet of cigarettes she holds.

Karen Let's get out of 'ere, Kim. Let's go for a walk or something. When I was walkin' up 'ere I 'eard a bit of reggae music. This car stereo quite a way off. Bloke 'ad 'is window open. Ain't nothin' really in the breeze. The breeze is really clean. So the music sort of like travelled.

Kim (*casual*) There's nothin' out there.

There is a banging on the door downstairs. They tense. Kim puts her cigarette out as if it has been a bomb alert. Another banging.

That's Mark.

Kim goes into the position that she was in at the beginning of the Act. Karen sits up alert.

Mark Kim. Ki-im. Kim. (*pause*) Kim. Ya in? Ya in? I'm

comin' up there, Kim. Ya ain't keepin' me . . . (*He tails off for a second, drunkenly.*) Kim. Ya fuckin' bitch. Ya fuckin' . . . I wan' see 'im. Kim. I kick the fuckin' door, I wan' see 'im, Kim. Ya can't keep me out. I fuckin' kick the door. I fuckin' . . . Kim . . .

There is silence for a while. Karen touches Kim's shoulder.

Karen You all right, Kim?

Kim's shoulder jumps but apart from that she stays still.

Mark 'E's my blood, Kim. 'E's my blood.'

Kim picks up the nearest thing to her and hurls it at the back wall.

I'm comin' up there, Kim. I wan' see 'im. I climb in the fuckin' winda. Kim. I'll climb in the fuckin' winda.

Kim Don't you fuckin' come up 'ere. Stay away, Mark, you 'ear me, stay away. I call the fuckin' police. Ya wan' him, do ya? You wan' Daniel, do ya? I frow 'im out the winda, shall I? I go get 'im, shall I? 'Cos you ain't comin' in 'ere. You fuckin' pisshead. Whaddya want from me, eh? Whaddya want from me? I'm calling the fucking police. (*She closes the window.*)

Mark (*his voice strained*) I wan' see 'im, Kim. I wan' see 'im.

Kim throws something else against the wall. There is a long pause.

Karen You all right, Kim?

Kim Yeah.

Karen I fink 'e gone.

Kim Yeah.

Karen Oy, Kim: ''E's my blood.'

Kim Stupid git.

Pause.

Karen Oy, Kim: 'Whadya want from me, eh? Whaddya want from me?'

They laugh.

'I'm throwin' 'im out the fuckin' winda.'

They laugh. Kim does a half-laugh half-cry.

Kim Stupid git.

Karen You all right, Kim?

Kim Yeah. (*She presses the intercom.*) Waaaa, Daniel.

Karen You gonna go inta him?

Kim He goes all stiff when I'm like this. Do you wanna go inta him, Karen?

Karen 'E's your son, Kim. (*Pause*) What ya thinking, Kim?

Kim I's jus' thinking about what you said about the christenin', about 'is presents.

Karen 'E ain't gonna know the difference if ya sell 'em. 'E ain't gonna know.

Kim Sometimes I think 'e knows everything.

Karen How?

Kim 'E jus looks like 'e knows everything sometimes. Like 'e knows.

Karen What ja mean?

Kim Sometimes 'e jus' looks up at me. I used to feel, like, what if I drop him, what if I just let him go an' drop him?

Karen Kim.

Kim It's just when you think, how am I gonna cope. With it all. Give me a fuckin' break.

Karen Our messes are ours, Kim. We gotta get ourselves out of 'em.

Kim I know and I'm gonna try, I really am. But sometimes I just think, what am I gonna do? With it all. If you scream help in this world you just hear it echoin' back to ya. Iss all right to scream help sometimes, innit?

Karen exits into the baby's room. Kim presses the intercom. We hear Karen's voice and the baby quietening.

Karen's voice Hello, little one. I'm your godmother, I am. Yeah. Shhh. I ain't never been a godmother before, have I? No. Shhh. There. I'm here 'cos Mummy ain't very well. She ain't feeling well, is she. No. Shhh. Shhh. There. Shh. All quiet now, innit. All quiet.

Karen comes back in with the baby.

Karen Eeyar, Kim. D'ya wanna take 'im?

Kim slowly accepts to take him.

Kim Hello, little one. What are your thoughts, eh? You don't 'ave any thoughts, do ya? (*feels his face*) Jesus, he's wet. (*She clasps him to her.*) You're so little, intcha. So little. (*She holds him up.*) What do ya see, eh? What do ya see?

Lights fade to black.

Afterword

I wrote *Essex Girls* while I was working as a youth drama worker in Grays. I grew up in Billericay, and memories of my school and people I knew then came back to life through writing.

The writing workshops run for the festival by the Royal Court Young People's Theatre gave me encouragement and support in developing my play. It was through seeing my work come alive that I got a stronger sense of the potential of the stage and I could experiment with ideas and see what was working dramatically. Opening up my work for discussion with other writers, directors and actors was inspiring.

Since the festival, the encouragement of the Royal Court Theatre has been vital to me too. I've completed a placement at the theatre and had further access to writing workshops and I've been supported in researching and writing a new play.

Essex Girls is indebted to the young women I met as a youth drama worker. I wish them the freedom to have in their hands what they hold in their hearts and I hope their imaginations will always run away with their beliefs!

Many thanks to Artspace, Grays, the Royal Court and the Royal Court Young People's Theatre. Also thank you to the following members of WAVES: Shelli Green, Keri Green, Laurie Collins, Natasha Daly and Kim Wallage, and to the girls in Ruth House, summer 1994.

Rebecca Prichard
April 1995

CORNER BOYS

Kevin Coyle

farholt ♡

Characters

Dave
Barry
Johnny (Jonathan Doherty)
Kerry Kerr
Angela
Tony Carey
Chopper
Bernie

Corner Boys was first performed at the Royal Court Theatre Upstairs in association with the Royal National Theatre Studio on 18 October 1994 with the following cast:

Dave Jonathan McGuinness
Barry Alan Maher
Johnny/Tony/Chopper Andy Snowden
Angela Nicola Stapleton
Kerry Faith Flint
Bernie Emma Owen Smith

Director Roxana Silbert

Act One

SCENE ONE

Lights come up exposing a street set. It is dark. A lamp post is giving the only light. Two boys run down from the audience to the stage, under the light.

Dave Good one. Hah, we showed them!

Barry What? How to run?

Dave Naw, a good fight. A great fight! (*He trots around under the light, acting macho.*)

Barry Yeah, but Chopper's big brother will kill us.

Dave Naw he won't. I could take him on easily.

Barry What about his gang, his Posse?

Dave (*punching Barry on shoulder*) Well, we've got our gang. Me and Tony'll pay a wee visit to Mr Morrow's house to talk about his wee brother.

Barry (*removing hand from shoulder*) Are you mad or something? First you try to get off with Chopper's girl and then you start a fight with him.

Dave I didn't try to pick up Donna, it was mutual attraction, she fancies me!

Barry (*sliding down lamp post*) Why'd she fancy a sad, pathetic dick like you?

Dave Well, Wendy didn't like you. She blew ye out. Ginger pubes, ginger pubes.

Barry Well, didn't we have a great night. First we're blown out and then we're bein' attacked by a bunch of E-heads.

251

Dave I wonder where the rest of the boys are, wouldn't they be in Maude's now?

Barry I don't know! Why don't you check?

Dave walks to rear right of stage. Looks at curtain.

Dave Aye, I see Johnny. (*looks at Barry*) Will I call him? (*loud roar*) Oi, Johnny, down here. It's me and Barry.

*Enter **Jonathan Doherty**, aged around sixteen, tall, pale. Dressed in Indy gear. Walks towards the guys from rear right.*

Johnny Hows about ye's!

Dave Did ye hear – me and Barry kicked Chopper's ass.

Johnny Like hell ye did! His gang would knife yous or something like that.

Barry Naw, they couldn't run as fast as us!

Barry and Johnny burst into laughter.

Dave Hah, bloody hah!

Johnny Why'd yous fight?

Barry Dave tried de' get off with Donna McFadden.

Johnny Are you mad or something? God, she's like Chopper's status symbol, she's his Reebox Pump, she is.

Dave She was on the pull! We were just flirting! There was no harm in it!

Johnny He's going de' get his brother Darren de' you! God, you're so dead.

Dave Naw, I'll sort it out. Me and Tony'll pay him a visit the morrow.

The group laugh.

Johnny (*serious tone*) Naw, Dave, be careful, they're mad. Remember what they did de Jack. He's still in a bad way. They're completely mad and they're getting worse.

Barry listens intently. Dave acts as if he knows it all.

(*after a pause*) I suppose you heard about Tony and his girly friend.

Barry What him and Bernie Quinn?

Johnny Ah! (*smug look*)

Barry and Dave What?

Johnny She's pregnant!

Dave Ah right! Jump in. (*He puts finger under eye and pulls skin down.*)

Johnny Seriously, she is.

Barry Who told you that?

Johnny Marty McDaid.

Dave I wonder whose legs will be broken the morrow night!

Johnny Well, don't tell him I told yous.

Both Naw, we won't!

Johnny Are yous coming up for chips? (*indicates with hand to rear right*)

Dave Naw, I have de' go! Barry, are you coming?

Barry Naw, I think I'll go up de' the chippy.

Dave All right, then. See yous. (*Walks offstage at the left.*)

Johnny Aren't you a kid!

Barry What?

Johnny Gon-ye-boy-ye!

Barry What are you talking about?

Johnny You and Kerry Kerr.

Barry What about me and Kerry Kerr?

Johnny Aren't you going out with her?

Barry No! (*looks puzzled then the penny drops*) Why? What have you heard about Kerry Kerr?

Johnny Oh, nothing!

Barry Come on, give.

Johnny A little bird told me she fancies you.

Barry Who's the little bird?

Johnny Can't say.

Barry Liar! (*dirty look from Johnny*) Come on! I want some chips.

The lights go down.

SCENE TWO

As Scene One, next day.

Barry What the hell are we waiting here for?

Dave To see Mr Morrow.

Barry (*look of shock*) What, Chopper's big brother? Are you serious?

Dave Ah, didn't we discuss it last night?

Barry I thought you were joking. He'll kill us.

Dave Naw, not if we describe the situation.

Barry You don't have to describe the situation, nothing happened. We annoyed Chopper and his mates, we ran like shit. He doesn't have to be involved.

Dave Aye, you're probably right.

Barry Course I am. If anything else happens we'll tell Chopper's big brother. But I don't think it'll do any good. He can't control Chopper, the drugs control Chopper.

Long pause, as these words sink into Dave.

After you left last night me and Johnny were talking.

Dave About what?

Barry Ah, a certain girl who fancies you.

Dave Who?

Barry Angela . . . Ye'know Angela, Jack's sister.

Dave (*untrusting look*) She fancies me?

Barry (*serious look, serious voice*) I heard she did. Guess what else I heard, ye'know Kerry.

Dave Aye, ye mean Kerry Kerr?

Barry Aye, she fancies me.

Dave (*look of smug, pompous satisfaction*) Sure I could a told you that.

Barry Well, why didn't ye?

Dave I thought you could see.

Pause as Barry shuffles about and fidgets.

Barry So what are we going to do about this?

Dave (*uneasy*) I suppose we could ask them out.

Barry How?

Dave Have ye never been out with a girl before?

Barry Course I have.

Dave Well, what did you do before?

Barry I got you to arrange it.

Dave Oh aye, so I did.

Pause.

Barry Well, what did you do?

Dave I got Johnny to arrange it.

Barry Well, this is great. Here we are, we're sixteen and we don't know how to ask a girl out.

Dave (*acting self-confident*) I'll just go up to them and ask them to go out with us.

Barry (*smirking*) Good, 'cos here they come now.

Enter two attractive girls, aged sixteen, highly feminine, dressed in equivalent styles to the boys. **Kerry Kerr** *is tall and blonde,* **Angela** *is tall and brunette. They are the same height as the lads. Remember, the lads are equally handsome/athletic but they lack confidence. They enter from rear left.*

Angela Hi, boys.

Dave All right Angela, Kerry, how's about yis?

Angela (*smiling*) Ach, fine, how's about yous?

Dave Same as usual.

Kerry (*to Barry*) I heard yous were mixing it with Chopper and his crowd last night.

Barry Aye, big man here started a fight.

Angela (*sarcastically*) Oh, big boy, did you sort them out?

Kerry (*sardonically*) Oh yes, my big hero.

Dave (*annoyed*) Ach, it was nothing. (*playfully*) I just beat them about the head with a frozen chicken.

Angela Don't mess with these boys. They're serious, look at what they did de my brother.

Barry Yeah, I know they're serious.

Kerry Aye, they're mad bastards, aren't they?

Long pause; everyone begins to fidget. Barry hits Dave with his shoulder, nudging him into action, or trying to; he has to hit him again.

Dave Are ye OK there, Barry?

Barry Naw, I felt like nudging you with my shoulder, is that all right with you?

Dave Aye, I suppose so.

Angela So where are yous off to . . . or are yous just loitering about scaring off us decent folk?

Barry (*joking*) What's decent about you pair?

Kerry So we're trash, are we?

Dave Did we say that?

Pause. Kerry looks at Angela. Barry looks at Dave.

Angela Well, I suppose we'll be seeing yous about.

Kerry Aye, see yous, bye.

Dave Aye, see you, Angela.

Barry Aye, see you, Kerry.

Dave See you, ye edjit, why'd ye do that.

Barry Why didn't you talk to them and ask them out?

Dave I don't know.

SCENE THREE

Street scene. Night time. Lighting as in Scene One. Dave and Barry are talking.

Dave Right, the girls will walk this way in a couple of minutes, right?

Barry (*enthusiastically*) Right!

Dave We then start to talk to them, right?

Barry Right.

Dave I ask Angela out on Saturday night and you ask Kerry out as well. Right?

Barry Yeah, right.

A sound from offstage. Barry looks to see who it is.

Aw, look, here comes Tony.

Enter **Tony Carey**, *a tall hard-man type, dressed in the same style as the lads.*

Tony All right, boys, how's it going?

Dave Same as usual, Tony, how's yourself?

Tony Same as usual.

Barry (*joking*) What, nothing new?

Tony Naw . . . What d'ye mean?

Barry Ah, well, there are some rumours about you and your wife.

Tony (*annoyed*) What d'ye mean?

Dave Certain people have said that Bernie's pregnant.

Tony Fuck off!

Barry Seriously, as your friends we have to tell you these rumours.

Tony When did ye hear, who told ye?

Dave (*gestures*) Last night, right here. Johnny Doherty told us Marty McDaid told him that your Bernie was preggers.

Tony Those bastards, I'll kill the fuckers.

Barry Aye, ye'd do, right. We'd a told ye before except that we haven't seen ye since yesterday morning.

Tony I'm going to go get them, be seeing ye.

Dave God, I wouldn't want to be those two! God, they are so dead.

Barry Serves them right for saying stuff like that.

Pause. They fidget, act bored, irritable. Barry looks off.

Look up – here come the girls!

Dave (*acting cool*) Right, here we go.

Enter Angela and Kerry slowly, wandering on stage. They point to the lads and walk over to them.

Angela All right, lads? What's up?

Dave Oh, nothing. (*posh accent*) Just standing about acting cool.

Kerry (*similar accent*) Oh, are we? How super.

Barry So what were you two up te de'day?

Angela Why do you want to know?

Barry I think it will help me in writing my book about teenage drama queens, their movements, virtues, vices and a, a, a sex lives.

Kerry (*sarcastically*) So you're interested in our sex lives?

Dave Oh, he's very interested in your sex life.

Kerry (*smiling*) Oh, are you? (*She puts hands on his shoulder, moves up and kisses Barry's ear.*)

Angela (*evilly*) Oh, poor baby got a reddener. (*She moves up to Barry and pulls his cheeks . . . facial that is.*)

Dave God, you must be in heaven, two beautiful women after your body, I wish I was you.

Angela Do you? Well, maybe you could.

Kerry Aye, didn't ye know Angela fancies your tight wee arse?

Barry That's OK. He wants her arse as well.

Angela So you don't like Kerry, do ye?

Barry I like her very much, so much so I would like to ask her out for a date.

Kerry (*stunned*) So ye do? What makes you think I'd want to go out with you?

Barry Because you like me and I like you.

Kerry OK. I would like such a date.

> *Barry and Kerry lock arms, look into each other's eyes lovingly.*

Dave (*shyly*) Ah, Angela, I really like you, do you want to go out with me a, a, a, some time?

Angela (*pausing to consider*) Well, why not? Yes, I'd be pleased to accompany you on a date.

Dave and Angela lock arms and look into each other's eyes.

Barry So, Kerry, where do you want to go?

Kerry I'd like to go to Kentucky Fried Chicken.

Barry Why?

Kerry So we could find out more about each other.

Barry All right then.

Dave So, Angela, where do you want to go?

Angela Just to a café for a cup of coffee.

Dave Why?

Angela So we can get to know each other.

Dave All right, then.

Girls When?

Boys Tomorrow night.

Girls Fine.

Boys Great.

The girls kiss the boys on the cheek and then exit.

Barry We're on to a winner there.

Dave Too right.

Act Two

SCENE ONE

A dining room or kitchen in Angela's home. Kerry and Angela sit talking to each other at the table.

Angela And then he said: 'You know, you're really beautiful, Angela.' Well, I just thought, Dave stop the bullshit, but I sat there and listened to him telling me all about my elegant profile.

Kerry Barry's just the same, he can spout some amount of dribble. He goes on about how beautiful I am and how he adores me. You know what's really funny?

Angela What?

Kerry I think he believes it.

Angela Lucky you, Dave only flatters me to try and have his evil way with me.

The girls giggle.

Kerry Naw. Barry's really sweet, he's a wee honey. It's just great the way he makes me feel like a goddess, or a queen or something.

Angela Yeah, well, whatever turns you on.

Kerry Well, I think my Barry's just about the best thing that's ever happened to me. We are getting on really well together and have such a great time. We are soul mates.

Angela Best thing! great time! soul mates! Yous two seem to be having a great time together, so come on, dish the dirt.

Kerry There's no dirt to dish. We have a pure love, unblemished by the unpure lusts of the hormonally challenged.

Angela (*laughing*) Yeah! good one.

Kerry So, come on, why don't you dish the dirt about Dave! Big Dave. (*She wiggles her little finger.*)

Angela Big Dave! Aye, he'd like to think so. He wants to be a big man, built like a body builder. He acts as if he was Mr Muscles but he's just my big cuddly teddy bear.

Kerry Ahhhhh, how sweet. So things are getting on well between you and Davey?

Angela Aye, everything's just great. Do you want a cup of tea or coffee?

Kerry I'll have a cup of coffee.

Angela I'll see if the kettle's done. (*She exits.*)

Kerry I suppose Dave has got wandering hands, always trying to get into your knickers.

Angela (*as she re-enters*) He only touches what I let him to. Mind you, he doesn't know what he's allowed to touch with his strong masculine hands.

Kerry (*laughing*) Oh! His strong dextrous masculine hands attached to his broad forearms. You dirty slut, you!

Angela (*laughing*) Yeah! Milk and two sugars, isn't it? (*She moves offstage.*)

Kerry Yes, please. Do you have any chocky bickies? I really like Barry. I think we should go out with them for a few more weeks.

Angela (*from offstage*) Yeah, about another two weeks!

Then we'll review the situation. You know what I always say: dump them before they dump you.

Kerry I think Barry's different.

> *Angela enters with two coffee cups and a packet of Penguins in her mouth. Kerry moves to intercept and takes a cup from Angela. They both sit down again and start to drink coffee and munch at chocolate biscuits.*

Angela Maybe he is, but Dave isn't anything really special!

Kerry You just described him as your big cuddly teddy bear.

Angela Yeah, well, maybe he is a bit more sensitive than other boys. But I'm not really sure if he's special.

Kerry Well, I think you know if he is or isn't.

Angela Said Kerry the junior psychologist! Knower of all our subconscious desires. Interpreter of dreams, reader of . . .

Kerry Seriously! You should be able to tell if he's special or not. You know how?

Angela (*singing*) Is it in his eyes?

Kerry No. And it's not in his kiss either.

Angela OK. Be like that!

Kerry Like what?

Angela I don't know. A minute ago you were having a laugh and now you're ripping my head off.

Kerry I didn't rip your head off. You're just too sensitive. Are you all right? Friends?

Angela Friends.

They clasp hands.

So are you and Barry going out the morrow night?

Kerry Aye, we might as well. Nothing better to do.

A clock strikes six.

Well, I better go. Me ma'll go spare. I'm already late for tea. (*She gets up to leave.*)

Angela Well, I'll see ye!

Kerry Yeah, bye. (*She exits stage left.*)

Angela Yeah, bye!

Lights down. Curtain closes.

SCENE TWO

Street scene, Barry is waiting at the lamp post. Barry looks annoyed, impatient. He glances at his watch several times. Dave wanders on.

Barry About time, where've you been?

Dave I was just talking to the girls.

Barry (*grooming himself*) Are they here?

Dave Naw, they're away down the town. So are you going to this disco tonight?

Barry What, the night club? Yeah, me and Kerry are going, are you and Angela going?

Dave Might as well, nothing better to do on a Saturday night. It's going to be good, isn't it?

Barry Yeah, should be. It's supposed to be dead hard to get into. You got your fake ID?

Dave Of course I have. I never leave home without it.

Barry So how are things getting on between you and Angela?

Dave Ye know how it is, we're just getting on fine, can't see enough of each other.

Barry Yeah, same here. I really like Kerry, she's real nice.

Dave Yeah, she's a great personality, nice-looking too.

Barry (*messing around*) Are you eyein' up my bird? I'll give you a thick ear, my son. You stick to your missus or I'll have to take my belt off to you.

Dave Oh, yeah?

> *Dave grabs Barry in a side lock; the fight is only in fun. Barry grabs Dave at the thigh and throws him up in the air. Dave lands on his feet and gets into a karate stance.*

(*oriental accent*) You have dishonoured my family – for this you must surely die.

> *Dave and Barry face each other as if to fight.* **Chopper** *enters on stage and stands watching the two friends circle. Chopper watches in interest. Barry and Dave start to wrestle. During this match Dave gets the upper hand as he is the biggest.*

Chopper Hello, boys. Having one of your jolly little queer embraces. I always wondered about your sexualities, always thought yous were swinging to the wrong side.

> *Dave is annoyed and breaks off from Barry and approaches Chopper.*

Dave Fuck off, Chopper, or I'll rip your fuckin' spleen out.

> *Barry holds Dave back.*

Chopper No, you won't. I'll kick your ass, fucking queer. Your Angie was good last night, she pumped me dry.

Dave launches himself at Chopper, the fight is quick and fast. Dave kicks him in the groin and head. Chopper staggers and then tries to punch Dave in the face. Dave blocks and knee strikes Chopper, who slumps to the ground.

Barry Jesus, Dave, we're dead now, his gang'll kill us.

Dave Fuck them. (*to Chopper*) You're nothing without your friends.

Chopper I'll get yous'ence, you're all dead.

Dave kicks Chopper in the chest.

Dave At least I got you first.

Dave and Barry exit.

Chopper I'll get yous, ye bastards.

Lights down.

SCENE THREE

Dave and Barry are standing at the corner lamp post. The boys are all dressed up; they seem to be anxious. Dave looks at his watch.

Dave They're fifteen minutes late, where the hell are they?

Barry Probably getting themselves dolled up. Women! Putting the war paint on, out to get a few scalps.

Dave Shut up, you prick.

Barry What's eating you?

Dave Nothing, why, what should be eating me?

Barry (*trying to appease*) Nothing, just calm down.

Dave I wish they'd hurry up, we'll be late and miss the start of the session.

Barry Don't worry, they'll be here. They don't want to miss the start of the gig . . . the crack will be ninety the night.

Dave Too right, see the Beats they rock, if they were vampires they'd be Rockula.

Barry Yeah they kick ass . . . Dave aren't you worried about what Chopper'll do to us. After all, ye did kick his head in.

Dave reflects on it and then smiles.

Dave Naw.

Barry But ye know he can't let us get away with what ye did. After what that dick Johnny told everyone.

Dave No, you see everyone's known for ages that he can't fight without his gang. People know anyone could beat him. I did it, I kicked his ass, his gang won't come after us, they'll want to see a rematch between me and him. You're safe and I'm safe, because if he comes up against me, I'll kick his ass.

Barry Dave, you talk the biggest load of shite I've ever heard. It'd make sense if Chopper's gang were, like, right in the head but as you and I know they're nothing more than E-heads.

Dave realizes that Barry speaks the truth, whether with forked tongue is open to conjecture.

Dave (*not smiling*) Eek. Ah, well, you win some, you lose some.

Barry Yeah, but not usually teeth. Dave, let's face it, we're fucked, they'll kill us.

Dave Aye, as long as they don't touch the girls.

Barry Yeah, too right, if they harm the girls they're dead.

Noise offstage and then the girls enter.

Dave Well, speak of the devil.

Angela Hi, lover, I wondered why my ears were burning.

Dave and Angela kiss.

Barry Hi there, sexy. (*He takes Kerry's hand and she slowly turns round.*) Why, you look fine, so good I gotta see it twice.

Kerry You look mighty fine yourself, big boy. Kiss me before I explode.

They kiss.

Dave So, are we going?

Barry Yeah, I don't see why not. Any objections, girls?

Angela Yeah, just one.

Dave What is it? Are yous OK?

Angela Yeah, of course we are. We just wanted to give yous a present.

Kerry Yeah, come with me, Barry.

Kerry takes Barry's hand and leads him to one side of the stage. They turn and face each other. Angela and Dave do likewise.

Boys What's our present?

Girls This, honey. (*The girls twist the boys' nipples.*)

Dave You're dead, ye bitch.

He grabs Angela and lifts her up. She laughs. Barry tries

to do the same to Kerry but she dances out of the way.

Kerry Got ye, big boy.

Barry Why you . . .

He grabs her and bear hugs her and she laughs.

Dave (*still holding Angela*) C'mon, Barry, let's go and see the show.

They exit carrying the girls and the lights dim.

SCENE FOUR

Street scene, daytime. Dave is standing, looks anxious, he is waiting for someone. He looks at his watch.

Dave Late as always. (*looking around*) Where is she?

Kerry enters.

Kerry How's about ye, Dave?

Dave I'm all right. How are you?

Kerry Pretty good. (*silence*) So what are you waiting for?

Dave Just Angela, we're going to the pictures.

Kerry Ahhh, that's nice, I'm here de' meet Barry, we're going down to see the fair.

Dave That's nice, me and Angela went last night, it's pretty good.

Kerry Yeah, so we've heard.

Silence. She looks offstage once more. Dave does likewise.

So you and Angela are getting on well?

Dave Yeah, brilliantly.

Kerry That's nice.

Silence.

Dave So, how're things between you and Barry?

Kerry Oh, they're ace.

Dave Yeah, everyone seems to be getting on well. Haven't seen you and Barry for a while.

Kerry We've been busy.

Dave Yeah, so've me and Angela. We must get together some time.

Kerry What me 'nd you? No thanks.

Dave Don't be stupid, me 'nd Angela, you 'nd Barry.

Kerry Don't call me stupid, ye ape.

Dave Shut up, ye slag.

Kerry Fuck you, ye bastard.

Barry walks on stage.

Barry Did I hear raised voices?

Kerry (*shooting a stare at Dave*) Naw, honey, we were just arguing over football.

Dave Who do you think'll win the FA Cup?

Barry Liverpool.

Dave In your dreams.

Barry Stranger things have happened.

Dave Yeah, I'm looking at one (*smiling at Barry*).

Barry (*laughs*) Now I can think of another. Anyway, we have de go or we'll be late.

Dave I know what ye mean. Angela is half an hour late. She should have been here at half seven.

Barry But, Dave, it's half seven now.

Dave Don't talk rubbish, look at me watch. (*He shows his watch.*)

Barry It's stopped.

Dave looks at watch.

Tell me, Dave, did you wind your watch this morning?

Angela walks on stage and approaches the group gathered around Dave's forearm.

Angela Darling, if you've got a tattoo I'll kill ye.

Kerry Naw, the big dill forgot de wind his watch this morning and he's been standing here for half an hour. He checked his watch every couple of minutes and it didn't get through his thick head that the little hand wasn't working.

Angela Is this true?

Dave C'mon, Angela, we gotta go to the cinema.

Angela OK. (*huffy*) See yous later.

Kerry Yeah, see ya, honey.

Dave walks off, dragging Angela behind him.

Jesus, that Dave is an ape, isn't he?

Barry Yeah, but he's all right, ye know, he's dead on.

Kerry Do I? He tried to pick me up before you came.

Barry Naw, he didn't. Dave isn't the type to go off with another man's girl.

Kerry What, am I branded as your woman?

Barry Naw, ye know what I mean.

Kerry (*looking Barry in the face*) Yeah, I suppose I do. Come on, Tarzan, take me to the fair.

Barry (*beating chest*) Come with me, Jane.

   Barry takes Kerry by the hand and they walk off.

Kerry (*while walking*) Barry.

Barry Yes, love?

Kerry You're not really a man, are you? (*She laughs.*)

Act Three

SCENE ONE

Angela's home, as in Act Two, Scene One. Angela is sitting reading a magazine. There is a knocking sound from offstage. Angela leaves and returns a few seconds later with another girl, **Bernie.**

Angela Come in, Bernie. What did you come about?

Bernie (*takes off coat and sitting*) It's about those two dickheads, Barry and Dave.

Angela gives Bernie a dirty look.

Angela Why? What have they done?

Bernie You heard that your Dave kicked the living Jesus out of Chopper about a week ago?

Angela He what?!

Bernie Didn't he tell you?

Angela doesn't reply.

He didn't, that useless git. Right, I'll tell you what happened in as few words as possible. (*She takes a deep breath.*) Right, a couple of weeks ago Dave tried to get off with Chopper's slag.

Angela He what?

Bernie Naw, it was before yous two were going out. Anyway, Chopper swore he'd kill Dave and Barry. Well, anyway, last week or maybe the week before Chopper started on your Dave, Anyway, Chopper said something about you and Dave kicked the living Jesus out of him.

274

During Bernie's speech Angela is enthralled and by the end of it her mouth is hanging open.

Angela He kicked the fuck out of Chopper? Well, that must be his martial arts training.

Bernie Yeah, him and Barry are black belts, aren't they?

Angela Naw, just blue.

Bernie Anyway, Chopper's supposed de have organized his gang and they're going de get Dave and Barry. Well, Dave heard about this and he's organizing all his mates de sort out Chopper's gang. Ye know, he wants a Mexican stand-off or a primitive strike or something like that.

Angela The idiots, that's the most stupid thing they could do. We've got to stop them.

Bernie Yeah, I know, but how'll we stop them?

Angela Next time I see Dave I'll tell him I'll dump him if he goes through with it. I'll get Kerry de do the same.

Bernie Well, I'll do the same de Tony. It's about all we can do, isn't it?

Angela Aye, suppose . . . But you can't really dump Tony, can ye?

Bernie Why not?

Angela Ah, nothing.

Bernie Ah, something . . . tell me why I can't dump Tony.

Angela I . . . ah . . . heard that you were pregnant.

Bernie What the fuck! I'm not pregnant. Where did you hear that?

Angela I heard that of Joan McClusky, the one who went out with Johnny Bigmouth.

Bernie Where did he come up with that? Tony. He must have told all his friends he'd shagged me! That bastard. I wouldn't even sleep with him. I'm still a virgin.

Bernie is now really angry and ready to kill someone. Angela is feeling rather sheepish and wishes she were somewhere else.

That's it, Tony can go and fuck himself. He's dumped. And I'm going be tell everyone how much of an inadequate bastard he is.

Angela Yeah, ye do right. If Dave gives me any trouble or gets in de a fight wi' Chopper when I'm around he can go fuck himself.

Bernie Yeah, too right.

Curtain closes, lights fade.

SCENE TWO

Street scene at night. Lamp post provides circle of light. Stage is empty, but talking and laughter from offstage. The two couples enter laughing. They are a little drunk.

Dave Aye, it was a good night, wasn't it?

Barry Sure it was. It was really great.

Kerry Yeah, we should do it more often.

Angela Yeah, let's do it next Friday.

Dave takes Angela's hand.

Dave Look, we'll see yous. I'll take Angela home.

Barry OK, we'll see yous.

Dave and Angela go to exit left but are suddenly

*blocked by people who appear from the darkness. The
four friends are suddenly surrounded by a gang of about
fourteen people, men and women.*

Angela (*distressed*) What the fuck's going on?

*Chopper appears and walks into the centre of the circle.
He acts as if he's on drugs. He acts hyper, possibly on
speed.*

Chopper Hi sexy. (*grabbing her shoulder*) How about me
and you party.

Angela Fuck off, ballbag.

Chopper Suit yourself.

*Chopper punches Angela in the face. Dave lunges at
Chopper and lays into him. Chopper's gang attack like
baboons. They get the four friends on the ground and
kick them in the heads. This 'fight' continues for two
minutes. Then they stop. The four friends are lying
bleeding.*

See yous, ye bastards. I want you to know, I'm king, I rule,
you're shite.

*Chopper kicks Dave in the head, then turns and walks
offstage. Some of his friends do likewise to the others on
the ground and then follow Chopper offstage. Pause.*

Dave (*crying*) Angela, are ye all right? (*Dave gets up. He
goes to Angela.*) Angela, Angela, wake up.

Lights fade, curtain closes.

SCENE THREE

*Several weeks have passed between this scene and the last.
Barry is sitting under the lamp post. He's wearing shorts*

and a T-shirt. He's listening to music and drinking Coke.
Dave walks on stage. He's dressed in shorts and a T-shirt.
He's wearing sunglasses.

Dave All right, Barry? Haven't seen you in a while.

Barry (*looking up*) Haven't been out in a while. So
how've you been?

Dave Mending. (*pause*) Me and Angela have split up, ye
know, after that night.

Barry (*pausing*) Yeah, same as Kerry and me. Said she
couldn't handle that sort of shite.

Dave Yeah, what'd the police say to you?

Barry Said it'd never stand up in court. No witnesses on
our side. They're bastards for gettin' away with that.

Dave Don't worry. We'll get them. Even if it takes us a
hundred years.

Barry Yeah, each one at a time.

Dave Yeah, we'll have our justice.

Barry You know what makes me angry about that night?
It's how ugly it all was. We didn't ask for it. It just
happened. And we had no control over the situation. But
that scum had.

Dave Yeah, it was really ugly. That Chopper, he'll get his.
We were the lucky ones. He has de be stopped before they
kill somebody.

Barry Yeah, we have to do something. We have to meet
him on his own terms, even though we don't want to do
it.

Dave Yeah. (*He stands.*) 'Mone, are ye going down the
park?

Dave stretches out his hand to Barry. Barry takes it and pulls himself up.

Barry Yeah, why not?

The two friends leave stage. Curtain closes.

Afterword

Corner Boys is my first play and I wrote it as an experiment. It reflects how I used to think and feel. Dave and Barry are derived from two distinct traits in my personality.

The boys hang around their corner because they have nothing else to do and nowhere else to go. That's exactly how most sixteen-year-olds from Derry feel. There are few facilities for them and they feel they can't do anything about it. So the lads just spend the summer wasting time by hanging around and acting cool. Then they hook up with Angela and Kerry. For the rest of the summer they enjoy themselves but unfortunately the fun can't last for ever. The fun's all over after an encounter with Chopper, a local hard man and part-time drug dealer.

I would like to thank all the people who were involved in the workshops held by the Royal Court writers. I owe special thanks to the staff of the Verbal Arts Centre in Derry, particularly Jim Craig. Praise is also owed to two teachers from my school: Eddie Mailey for showing me what it means to act, and Liam Burns for teaching me to read between the lines. Most of my gratitude is owed to the people who staged *Corner Boys* – the actors, stage management and most notably the director.

Kevin Coyle
May 1995